NOTES ON
EARLY SPANISH MUSIC

Da Capo Press Music Reprint Series

GENERAL EDITOR

FREDERICK FREEDMAN

VASSAR COLLEGE

CRITICAL AND BIBLIOGRAPHICAL NOTES ON EARLY SPANISH MUSIC

By Juan F. Riaño

DA CAPO PRESS · NEW YORK · 1971

A Da Capo Press Reprint Edition

This Da Capo Press edition of
*Critical and Bibliographical Notes on
Early Spanish Music* is an unabridged
republication of the first edition published
in London in 1887.

Library of Congress Catalog Card Number 79-158958
SBN 306-70193-6

Published by Da Capo Press, Inc.
A Subsidiary of Plenum Publishing Corporation
227 West 17th Street, New York, N.Y. 10011

Critical and Bibliographical

NOTES

ON

EARLY SPANISH MUSIC.

Critical & Bibliographical

NOTES

ON

EARLY SPANISH MUSIC.

By JUAN F. RIAÑO,

MEMBER OF THE ROYAL ACADEMIES OF HISTORY AND OF FINE ARTS OF MADRID.

WITH NUMEROUS ILLUSTRATIONS.

LONDON

BERNARD QUARITCH, 15 PICCADILLY.

M.DCCC.LXXXVII.

LONDON :
WYMAN AND SONS PRINTERS, GREAT QUEEN STREET,
LINCOLN'S-INN FIELDS, W.C.

CONTENTS.

————

LIST OF ILLUSTRATIONS.

———•◦•———

PREFACE.

THE *Gaceta Musical de Madrid* published thirty years ago, in its number of the 18th of March, a quotation from M. Adrian de la Fage, in which he says : "How numerous are the difficulties and how obscure is the history of music, and how many points remain yet to be cleared up ! . . . . A proof of this is the almost complete ignorance which we are in concerning the ancient school of Spanish music before Palestrina."

These words of the French critic are applicable to the present day, for modern authors who have written on the subject barely allude to musical annotations or compositions by Spanish authors. This causes a sad break in the history of musical art; it is justified in a measure by the silence of Spaniards themselves, who have hitherto shown little interest in collecting materials for a complete history of Spanish music from the earliest times.

This reason has induced me to think that a real service will be done by facilitating information to those who have undertaken the study of music in the Middle Ages in Spain. I have collected the bibliographical information in the different libraries to which I have had access, so that students may be aware of the existence of a great number of Spanish manuscripts from the tenth to the sixteenth century which have musical annotations. I also give a catalogue of early-printed books on music up to 1600 by Spanish authors, which, owing to their extreme rarity, are bibliographical treasures, and constitute a group of works of the greatest interest for the history of the development and progress of European music in the Middle Ages and beginning of the Renaissance.

The names of Spanish painters, sculptors, and architects are well known out of the country, thanks to Ford, Stirling, Viardot, Layard, Street, Curtis, and many others ; thanks to them, Velazquez, Murillo, Berruguete, Alonso Cano, Herrera, and Juan de Toledo are popular and familiar to every civilised country. Spanish musicians, on the contrary, are hardly ever alluded to in any modern publication. Even in Félix Clément's " Histoire de la Musique," 1885, in the " Résumé Nominal " (chap. xxiv. p. 789), in which he gives a list of composers, theoretical writers and musical historians, not a single Spanish musician of the fifteenth century is mentioned, and the names of only two of the sixteenth are given, Guerrero and Victoria. There is not a word on Spanish books on music, or the music composed during these two centuries, although these works are by far superior to those on the kindred arts. Barely a dozen authors of any importance have written in the sixteenth and seventeenth century on painting, sculpture, and architecture, while more than fifty have done so on music, some with great judgment and discretion.

There are very few examples of painters, sculptors, or architects who have emigrated from Spain, while musicians in large numbers are known to have settled in Italy in the fifteenth and sixteenth centuries and competed with the best masters of the time. Some idea may be formed of this by referring to Don Francisco Asenjo Barbieri's " Discurso " at the Royal Academy of San Fernando. (Madrid, 1874.)

The learned writer tells us that during the lifetime of Lorenzo de Medici, a professor of music of the University of Salamanca, called Bartolomé Ramos de Pareja, went to Italy and founded at Bologna a musical professorship ; he printed in 1482 a didactic work in which he developed his new theory of *temperamento*, which produced a most important revolution in the art of music.

The Spanish composer Cristobal Morales belonged in the first half of the sixteenth century to the Sixtine Chapel; the Italian author Adami da Bolsena, says he was a marvel of art. He composed a number of musical works before the time of Palestrina, which must have been very popular, for in Italy alone thirteen editions appeared in the same century. There are six editions of the same century of the works of another Spanish composer who was no less celebrated, who also belonged to the same Chapel—Tomás Luis de Victoria.

Juan de Tapia, a Spanish musician, by begging from door to door, collected a sufficient sum to found in Naples in 1537 the Conservatorio della Madonna di Loreto, the first school of music, which has been the model of all similar institutions since created in Europe. Upwards of thirty Spanish composers flourished in Italy during the sixteenth century, as Adami da Bolsena ("Observazioni per ben regolare il coro della Capella Pontificia") and Schelle ("die Päpstliche Sängerschule in Rom genannt die Sixtinische Capelle") tell us.

Their names are as follows:—

Juan Escribano.
D. Juan Palmares (Palomares ?).
D. Pedro Perez.
D. Blas Nuñez.
Antonio Ribera.
Juan del Encina.
Bernardo Salinas.

Geronimo Ardujeo (?).
Antonio Calasanz, de Lerida
Cristobal Morales.
Bartolomé Escobedo.
Pedro Ordoñez, tesorero de la Capilla
Francisco Talavera.
Esteban de Toro.
Juan Sanchez de Tineo.
Francisco Montalvo.
Francisco Bustamante.
Juan Sanchez.
Antonio Villadiego.
Francisco Torres, de Priora, toledano.
Francisco Soto, de Langa, diocesis del Burgo de Osma.
Juan de Figueroa.
Cristobal de Ojeda.
Tomas Luis de Victoria, de Avila.
Tomas Gomez, de Palencia.
Juan de Paredes, saguntino.
Gabriel Carleval, de Cuenca.
Juan Santos, toledano.
Diego Vazquez, de Cuenca.
Francico Espinosa, toledano.
Pedro Montoya, de Coria.

It is not my intention to praise Spanish musicians and far less to discuss their scientific theories. I confine myself to giving an account of the Spanish musical MSS. of the Middle Ages and early printed books, and some observations which I consider interesting relative to Visigothic *neums* which have never been appreciated by any author who has written on the subject.

The history of music in Spain begins with San Isidoro (VII cent[y.]). In the second book of his "Etimologiarum" he defines music in the following manner: "Musica est disciplina quæ de numeris loquitur, qui ad aliquid sunt his qui inveniuntur in sonis."

In the third book of the same work, "De Musica," he devotes the following nine chapters to the subject :—

"De musica et ejus nomine " ....chap. xv.
"De inventoribus ejus" .... „ xvi.
"Quid possit musica " .... „ xvii.
"De tribus partibus musicae" .... „ xviii.
"De triformi musicae divisione" .... „ xix.
"De prima divisione musicae quae harmonica dicitur" .... „ xx.
"De secunda divisione quae organica dicitur"... „ xxi.
"De tertia divisione quae rhythmica nuncupatur" „ xxii.
"De musicis numeris" .... „ xxiii.

San Isidoro does not allude to musical annotations, but describes the following instruments: Organum, Tuba, Tibia, Fistula, Sambuca, Pandura, Cithara, Psalterius, Lyra, Tympanum, Cymbala, Sistrum, Tintinnabulum, Symphoniam.

In another part of his works, entitled "de Officiis," he speaks of "De choris," "de canticis," "de psalmis," "de hymnis," "de antiphonis," "de lectoribus," and "de psalmistis." ("Divi Isidori, Hispal. Episcopi, Opera," 1 vol. fol. Madrid, 1599.)

San Isidoro was chiefly a compiler of science and classical literature, not, as is supposed by many, an original author. He was able to extract many MSS. which have disappeared since his time. In his theories on music, he appears to have followed exclusively the system of Boëtius. For this reason, he has been considered the author of the ancient mode of chant used in Spanish churches ; others affirm that it was invented by San Eugenio. The words which describe the music of this period are *Isidoriano, Eugeniano, Visigodo, melodico,* and *Muzarabe* or *Mozarabe* chants. *Melodico* is in contraposition to *Gregoriano,* and *Muzarabe,* because its method had been preserved by the Christians living in towns under the domination of the

Moslims ; these Christians were known by the name of
Muzarabs, which means "Arabes non puri, sed gentes
inter Arabes habitantes et cum iis conjuncti." (Freytag,
"Dicc.")

The ritual *Eugeniano* has, thanks to this, existed during
the domination of the Mahometans in Spain. When Toledo
was conquered by King Alfonso VI. in 1085, the Roman
or Gregorian breviary substituted it in the greater part of the
churches of the Peninsula, owing to the principal ecclesiastical appointments having been conferred on French monks
who used the Roman ritual. This was not brought about
without great difficulties, for the mass of people, accustomed
as they were to the tradition of the Visigothic or Muzarabic
ritual, rose in Toledo, and, as we read in the chronicles, it
was granted to them that both rituals should be submitted
to a holy ordeal. A combat took place in the Vega of
Toledo between two champions; the proof of fire was made,
and the rituals were both thrown into the flames, the
Visigothic one emerging triumphant. The king, notwithstanding, decided in favour of the Gregorian breviary,
although he gave permission that, in some churches in
Spain, the Muzarabic ritual should be allowed to continue.
This custom, which was favoured by Cardinal Ximenes de
Cisneros, in the sixteenth century, and other archbishops
who succeeded him, continues in the present day. There
is a chapel in the Cathedral of Toledo, in which the Muzarabic service is daily performed, the necessary *personnel*
of clergy and musicians are devoted exclusively to this
ritual, which continues exactly the same as in the Middle
Ages. The ceremonial is taken from old manuscripts,
but the music has suffered since then radical reforms in
its annotation, as well as in the theory and practice of
the chant. To discover what this music originally was,
is a problem which modern students are called upon to

resolve ; the study of the manuscripts which exist with Visigothic *neums* will be of great help towards this.

From the seventh to the end of the twelfth century, tradition has handed down to us the names of several important persons who distinguished themselves by their musical compositions ; besides San Isidoro and San Eugenio, already referred to, we have, Pedro, Bishop of Lerida ; Juan, Bishop of Zaragoza ; San Fulgencio ; San Leandro ; Tonancio, Bishop of Palencia; and Salvus, abbot of the monastery of Albelda. In the monastery of Ripoll (Cataluña) there existed formerly a Latin poem on music, composed in the eleventh century by a monk named Oliva, which is supposed to have been a composition founded on Boëtius's book (Villanueva, " Viaje Literario," Valencia, 1821, tom. viii. p. 57). It is probable that the music written by these authors accommodated itself to the system and tonality of the Visigothic chant, for the greater part of the Spanish musical MSS. which have reached us up to the twelfth century are written with Visigothic *neums*.

This love of tradition constituted in Spain almost an historic law, but during the eleventh and twelfth centuries there may be distinctly traced in the Spanish Fine Arts a direct and immediate French influence, which reached Spanish music, and must have produced a period of transition before it became submitted to the new schools which were imported from France and other parts of Europe. This, as I have already observed, was brought about by the number of monks of Cluny who came to Spain, and to whom the highest ecclesiastical posts were given. It must not be forgotten that, after the conquest of Toledo in 1085, the Roman breviary was imported by the French, and the Gregorian chant was the only one officially recognised by the Church. This French influence continues without interruption during the Middle Ages, and from the thirteenth century the *neums* and other signs which are to be found in Spanish MSS. are similar to the French ones.

Among the numerous works of Raimundo Lull, a native of Mallorca (1235), is " Ars Magna," which treats of different subjects. In the chapter, " Arbor Scientiae," he speaks of music in the following manner : " Musica est ars inventa ad ordinandum multas voces concordantes in unum cantum, sicut multa principia ad unum finem." Lull's musical system is explained in detail by the commentators of his works, in the edition which appeared at Mayence in 1721 (" Beati Raimundi Lulli Opera," etc., 10 vols. in fol.; the seventh and eighth were not published). If the explanation given is exact, we may infer that he modified with advantage the musical theories of Guido d'Arezzo ; but Lull's study, like San Isidoro's, is more the work of a philosopher than an artist, it belongs to the didactic or scientific school. The celebrated " Cantigas " by King Don Alonso el Sabio (thirteenth century) is one of the most interesting collections of practical music of its time.

The " Cantigas de Santa Maria " consist of 401 poems written on devotional subjects in Gallego dialect ; they were composed for singing, and each of them has a different music. The melodies are written with the key of *do* and *fa* on all the lines ; sometimes with a flat, sometimes without. Tradition supposes that the king himself was the author of the poems and the music ; but, as other works which have appeared with his name have been proved to be written by the learned men that he so generously protected, it is highly probable that the " Cantigas " are simply a compilation of songs of the thirteenth century, written by different composers ; this will doubtless be ascertained when the melodies are deciphered, but the king will always have the merit of having collected and known how to appreciate what otherwise would have been irretrievably lost. The three manuscripts which have reached us of the "Cantigas" are most interesting, not only on account of their poetry and music, but also owing to the splendid illuminations they contain. There are innumerable figures playing on different instruments ; facsimiles of fifty of the most interesting ones are given from the most important of these manuscripts (*vide* Appendix).

As no study has yet been made of the names of these instruments (because the "Cantigas" have never been published), it may be useful to refer to a poem by the Arcipreste de Hita, a poet of the fourteenth century, in which he names about thirty musical instruments used in his time (*vide* Appendix).

Manuscripts with musical notes have reached us of the fourteenth century; we find also in the " Leges Palatinas " of Don Jaime III de Aragon (*vide* Appendix) that musicians were employed in the king's service before his time ; they are mentioned in accounts of the household of Don Sancho, the son of Don Alfonso el Sabio (1296). Hitherto no didactic work on music of the fourteenth century has been found ; we must look for them in the second half of the fifteenth.

In Padre Villanueva's " Viaje Literario," already quoted (tom. xiv. p. 176), he mentions a treatise, " De Musica Instrumentali," composed in Barcelona by Fernando del Castillo, the Cuchillero, (lo Rahoher in Catalan); he tells us himself that he wrote it in 1497. This manuscript formerly belonged to the Capucine convent of Gerona ; its whereabouts is no longer known. Another manuscript was bound up with this one, " De pulsatione Lambuti et aliorum similium Instrumentorum," which was supposed to

have been written by a Moor of the kingdom of Granada,
called Fulan. We find at the end of it the following note:
"Omnia ista de pulsatione lambuti, ego habui a fratre
Jacobo Salvá ordinis Predicatorum filio den Bernoy de
Linariis diocesis Barchinone, qui charitate devinctus
revelavit mihi ista."

I have mentioned these manuscripts that they may be
known and looked for in the library of some collector, but
printed books of an earlier date exist which are of much
greater importance. Such are the works, "De Musica,"
by Bartholomé Ramos de Pareja (1482), "Lux Bella,"
by Domingo Marcos Duran (1492), "De Proprietatibus
Rerum," by Fray Vicente de Burgos (1494), and Guillermo
Podio's "Ars Musicorum" (1495). The golden age of
Spanish music begins with these authors, and, as I do not
intend to comment or discuss the works of Spanish musicians, but simply to give an idea of what they have published, I end here my historical account of Spanish music
before the Renaissance. An idea of the history of this
second period will be had by looking through the biblio-
graphy of early books on music by Spanish authors which
accompanies this Introduction.

I have added to this list another of the manuscripts
with musical notes which I know to exist in Spain. Such
a list appears now for the first time ; I not only consider
it of the highest interest that these manuscripts should be
known, but I expect that those possessing Visigothic
neums will cause many theories hitherto established to be
modified concerning the musical signs used in the Middle
Ages. I describe and give facsimiles of the most important
of the eighty manuscripts dating from the tenth to the
fourteenth century. The fine choir-books of the Escurial
or Cathedral of Seville are not included: the music they
contain is not sufficiently varied to require a special

description, although they number in all more than four hundred volumes. It is most probable that other musical manuscripts of the Middle Ages exist in Spain, hidden away in churches and other places of the kind. This Catalogue is followed by an Appendix of the documents of different kinds which illustrate the history of musical annotations and musical instruments.

The only two modern Spanish works which have appeared in Spain on music are, "Historia de la Musica Española desde la Venida de los Fenicios hasta el año de 1850," by Mariano Soriano Fuertes (4 vols. 4°, Madrid, 1885), and "Historia de las Ideas Estéticas en España," by Don Marcelino Menendez y Pelayo (3 vols. 8°, Madrid, 1883). The first of these works is written with little criticism, especially in the study of music in the middle ages ; Soriano is obscure and deficient in accurate information : the second is by far superior, it is an admirable study as far as it goes, but he only gives the names of thirty printed books of the early period, while I double the number.

As I consider Visigothic *neums* so important, I will make some remarks upon their study, which I consider interesting, beginning with an explanation of their paleographical character.

More than twenty years ago, Don Manuel de Goicoechea, librarian of the Royal Academy of History of Madrid, informed me that he had discovered a close connexion between the signs of Muzarabic or Visigothic music and certain characters of small letters (*cursivae*) sometimes used in signatures of documents of the tenth, eleventh, and twelfth centuries. Later on, in 1867, Don José Foradada published an article on this subject with facsimiles in "El Arte en España" (tom. vi. p. 105, Madrid), but both these authors merely discussed the problem under a paleographical point of view. Nobody has since, to my knowledge, continued these investigations.

By a minute examination of the signatures of the manuscripts mentioned by Señor Goicoechea, and comparing the letters, which are always small or *cursivae*, with the Visigothic *neums* of different manuscripts, the result undoubtedly appears to be that the musical Visigothic annotation is composed of :

(α) letters belonging to this special alphabet.

(β) of accents, points, and other purely musical signs.

(γ) of combinations of these signs with these letters.

At first sight, the *neums* appear as if they could easily be deciphered ; but, notwithstanding this, the music is not easily read, nor can it be transposed to modern notes. More competent judges than I are of the same opinion.*

The musical Visigothic annotations are so curiously formed, that they do not at first sight appear to be letters at all. The only manner of ascertaining that they are letters is by comparing them with the different fac-similes (*vide* Appendix) of the signatures of contemporary documents which I have already mentioned. By doing this, the connexion between them is apparent, and the similarity of many of the signs met with in the text. The reason of this similarity in the case of an alphabet which was so little in use can only be explained by attributing its use to a traditional custom, which it is difficult in the present day to trace. The principal difficulty arises from the fact that there are very few manuscripts of an earlier date than the tenth century, and in none of these are any music or signatures with these ciphered characters to be found : this prevents us from

* Don Francisco Asenjo Barbieri, Conde de Morphy, and Don Mariano Vasquez.

knowing what the early *neums* originally were. Manuscripts of the tenth, eleventh, and twelfth centuries are very
numerous with or without music ; our arguments, therefore,
must be confined to these three centuries.

The form of letter used by the Visigoths, before their
monarchy was destroyed in the eighth century by the
Arabs, was used by the Christians, with some few excep-
tions, until the end of the twelfth century, in which the
French manner of writing was introduced. Visigothic
characters may be divided in two groups—common
writing, and cipher :

(α) Capital letters (*magistrales*), used in manuscripts ;
and small letters (*cursivae*), employed in public or
private documents.

(β) Documents written in cypher, of which three different kinds are known.

A sufficient number of documents illustrating these
groups will be found in "Paleografia Visigoda," by Don
Jesus Muñoz y Rivero (Madrid, 1881, p. 77). Three
systems of cipher existed :—

(i) To substitute vowels by points or by some of the
letters representing Roman numbers.

(ii) To write Latin words with Greek characters.

(iii) To use a special alphabet different to any other
known, a few of the letters of which have some
similarity to the Visigothic small (*cursivae*) letters.

This alphabet is the one used for music; it is supposed
to have been derived from the old Roman *cursiva*
character (*vide* this Alphabet in Appendix copied from
Señor Muñoz's "Paleografia").

Two curious facts must be observed, to which attention
must be drawn : 1st, that these letters were invariably
used in musical manuscripts, and in signatures during the
tenth, eleventh and twelfth centuries; in the thirteenth

they disappear at the same time in both cases ; 2nd, that in the "Antiphonary of Montpellier," and other contemporary examples in which the whole system of alphabetical annotation appears, the same letters are found in the music as in the text, while in Spanish Visigothic manuscripts the letters are represented by a differently ciphered alphabet. The only reason I can give to explain this is the traditional custom of writing music in this manner without any reference to the forms of letters used in the texts of the manuscripts ; and, although the doubt occurs whether musicians transcribed their music merely by signs without reference to its alphabetical value, it seems probable that they did not ignore the cipher, as it was used simultaneously by the high clergy and men of letters who exclusively had to intervene in this kind of music.

My opinion is that the *neums* which are to be found in Visigothic musical manuscripts derive their origin from an earlier date than the tenth century ; we may even suppose that the same system was extended and carried into practice in other different countries where it was set aside much before it was in Spain, where it continued to be used until the end of the twelfth century. I believe that, in this century, and perhaps in the previous one, Visigothic *neums* were in use only in the Spanish peninsula, and that they were unknown elsewhere ; at any rate, they were not familiar to the monks of Cluny, learned as they were in matters of music. The interesting manuscript (F, 224) at the Library of the Royal Academy of History, which belonged at the end of the tenth century (or beginning of the eleventh) to the monasterio de San Millan, makes this fact most palpable. This monastery was occupied during the twelfth century by friars proceeding from Cluny, and when they found this manuscript so necessary for the ceremonies of the church, it is to be inferred that the Visi-

gothic *neums* were unknown to them, for they erased the
music of the Antiphons of daily use, and substituted the
Visigothic signs by *neums* of points similar to those used
in France at the same period. We find in this manuscript,
incomplete as it is, fourteen erasures in which the music has
been substituted by the French points; it is of great interest
that one of the anthems has been left with the two musical
annotations ; this circumstance may be useful for the interpretation of the music. Three facsimiles are given
which will illustrate this point.

In comparing the *neums* of Visigothic music with other
contemporary musical annotations, which have been given by
authors who have written on the subject, some resemblance
appears at first sight between them. In the signs of Greek
musical annotation which mark the measure of time, and in
others of greater importance called ἱποστάσης, three or four
forms are met with which are similar to some of the Visigothic *neums* (Fetis, "Hist. de la Mus.," vol. iv. pp. 43 et
seqq.) ; they vary, however, in their relative positions, and
may perhaps be connected with the value that they represent. In the explanation of the Greek method by means
of its alphabet given by David and Lussy ("Hist. de la
Not.," p. 27), they consider the Greek *kappa* (*x*) as a
complementary sign and characteristic of the *third fourth;*
it must be stated here that in Visigothic *neums* the *c*
frequently appears in its natural form or in this manner, *x*,
similar to the Greek *kappa*. This same *c* either in its
natural form or inverted is also to be met with in Armenian
annotation (David and Lussy, pp. 66, 67). In looking
through the tables of *neums* published by different
authors, it appears at first sight that a number of the signs
are similar to those of the Visigoths, but very few have
any resemblance with them. I consider that the best and
most complete tables are given in the works of Hugo

Riemann ("Studien zur Geschichte der Notenschrift)," and
in the Rev. P. Pothier's "Les Mélodies Grégoriennes";
from these tables the following signs may be considered
to have a certain resemblance with some of the letters of
the Visigothic cipher : *scandicus, epiphonus, quilisma,
podatus, salicus, trigon,* and *porrectus.*

Where the closest resemblance is to be found with the
Visigothic *neums* is in the "Gradual de Saint Gall,"
generally called the "Antiphonaire de Saint Grégoire,"
and in the "Antiphonaire de Montpellier." Both these
manuscripts have been the source of most heated discussions amongst musical critics. The authors who have
discussed this subject consider these manuscripts to belong
to the tenth or beginning of the eleventh century (Fetis,
tom. iv. pp. 207, 223 ; David and Lussy, p. 54). No
author has hitherto suspected the possibility that any
connexion should exist between the musical signs of these
manuscripts and the Visigothic *neums,* but by looking at
the facsimile published by Fetis, which begins, "Ostende
nobis . . . . . ." which is taken from the "Gradual de
Saint Gall," small points may be observed which are
undoubtedly musical signs and are similar to the Visigothic
ones; among them I believe I have discovered the
following six letters of the ciphered Visigothic alphabet :

(*c–e–i–m–n–t*). By examining also the facsimile given
by Fetis of the "Antiphonaire de Montpellier," which
begins, "Puer natus est nobis," it seems to me that other
six letters will be found, three of them are very clear

(*l–o–s*) and three more doubtful

(*i–p–t*). This study can never be

successful unless made on the manuscripts themselves or on good photographic facsimiles of the same, for I fear the letters may lose part of their character by being reproduced by engravings. There is no doubt that in the manuscripts of Saint Gall and Montpellier the Visigothic cypher is an important element; and this circumstance induces me to think that this manner of writing music must have been general in Europe in the tenth century, and that these manuscripts and the Visigothic ones proceed from the same source.

Some authors who have distinguished themselves in these studies are inclined to deny the importance of the letters used in musical annotation. I think that Coussemaker was the first to say this in his " Mémoire sur Hucbald"; his idea has met with numerous supporters. The Rev. P. Dom Joseph Pothier says that the form of the *neums* "n'a de rapport avec les caractères d'aucun alphabet" ("Les Mél. Grég.," p. 31); that the musical annotations in which seven or fifteen of the first letters of the alphabet are to be found, are purely didactic, and were only written for the use of the schools (p. 25); lastly, explaining his idea that he considers the Antiphonary, "comme un livre, non de choeur mais d'école," and discussing the system of Herman Contract (pp. 28, 29), he says that "les lettres à lui déterminent non les degrés de l'échelle, mais les intervalles que la voix doit franchir en allant d'une note à l'autre." In my opinion he is right in this as in many other points of his interesting book, but in some of his ideas there is evidently great exaggeration. David and Lussy (" Hist. de la. Not. Mus.," p. 43) admit these théories, and Felix Clément, in his " Histoire de la Musique" (p. 256), goes even further when he says: " Cette sorte de préférence donnée aux neumes a sa source dans le sentiment musical des accents combinés avec le rhythme, que les lettres n'exprimaient pas."

I have examined with the greatest care the Visigothic *neums* in the facsimiles which accompany this study, and find in them the following letters :

b–c–d–e–f–g–i–l–m–n–o–p–s–t–r.

The *p* only appears once (in the Manuscript of Toledo (32, 2), but I find a sign often repeated in the facsimiles which I suspect represents an *r.* I by no means consider this interpretation to be the right one ; but, as there is no doubt that these letters are to be found in the manuscripts, more competent students may be able to clear up this point.

We find here a system of mixed annotation composed of letters and *neums* similar to the one adopted by Hermann Contract in the eleventh century. A specimen taken from a manuscript of the Royal Library at Munich was published by David and Lussy in their "Hist. de la Mus.," p. 76. I do not find the same resemblance between them and the other annotations of single letters which are discussed by different authors, such as Hucbald's method, Odon de Cluny's, Reginon's, the two or three annotations published by anonymous authors, and, lastly, the one discovered by M. Nisard ("Revue Archéologique," 1852). All these methods are contemporary with those that appear in the Visigothic manuscripts ; the difference between them is that the letters are exclusively used without a combination of *neums.*

The fifteen or sixteen letters which I find in Visigothic music suggest to me a direct connexion with the Greek system, with Boetius's, or any other contemporary one, such as Odon de Cluny's, who, in the tenth century, settles the tone of the fifteen diatonic tones which form the two octaves by adopting a formula by which sixteen letters are included in the same way as in the Visigothic system.

I set aside these discussions, as I do not consider that the facts I have collected are sufficient to establish a fundamental system. I must mention two small Spanish works which were written for the purpose of interpreting Visigothic musical *neums;* one by Don Francisco Fabrian y Tuero, Canon of the Cathedral of Toledo, Bishop of Puebla de los Angeles (Mexico); the other by Don Geronimo Romero. Extracts from both these works will be found in the Appendix ("Missa Gothica, Breviarium Gothicum ").

The first of these studies is unknown to the modern authors who have written on music. Romero's study has been extracted and quoted by Fetis ("Hist. de la Mus.," vol. iv. pp. 194, 265); both these authors carry out a system of interpretation, which is founded on the traditional system of the Cathedral of Toledo of chanting this music from the earliest times. This enables these authors to establish the differences which they think ought to exist between the Gregorian and Visigothic melodies, *Eugenianus,* as Romero calls them, and also obliges them to explain, and give value to Visigothic *neums.* I am not sure they are right in their theories, but there is no doubt that they must not be passed by without notice; they are, besides, a faithful representation of Spanish traditions. Bishop Tuero publishes an example roughly copied from a fragment of Visigothic music, and, considering it as a type, he practically interprets (*vide* Appendix) each of the signs represented, and places them in the key to which they correspond. The chapel-master Romero developes his theory, which consists of four rules explaining the value of Visigothic musical signs, and establishes a system of proportion of time and musical measures. Fetis does not consider the system a perfect one: but, even as it stands, he thinks it of great importance when he says : " Ainsi se trouve éclairci un des points les plus obscurs dans l'histoire de la musique, et nous avons acquis la certitude que l'origine de cette notation proportionelle du Moyen Age sur laquelle tant d'erreurs se sont répandues, se trouve dans les neumes Saxons ou Gothiques et Lombards" (p. 271). Fetis insists on calling these musical annotations by the name of Lombard (pp. 186, 187), exaggerating, in my opinion, the Gothic influence of the first period of the Middle Ages, and forgetting the classical elements which may at the same time have formed them.

I have nothing to add to these observations, for my object is fulfilled by making known the ciphered alphabet, which is the principal element of Visigothic music, and giving the theories that I think may be useful for its interpretation. Before ending, however, it is necessary that I should make a special mention of the eminent Spanish composer, Don Francisco A. Barbieri; without his valuable help it would have been perfectly impossible to me to make this study. Señor Barbieri possesses the most extensive information on all matters connected with musical literature and art, especially on ancient Spanish music; he has the finest musical library in Spain, and has collected a great number of copies of manuscripts and historical notices which are most precious for the history of music. Señor Barbieri, with the generosity which characterises him, has placed all these materials at my disposal, and I am most happy to be able to express my gratitude towards him.

MANUSCRIPTS CONTAINING MUSICAL ANNOTATIONS.

MANUSCRIPTS OF THE Xᵀᴴ OR XIᵀᴴ CENTURY.

I.

Gothic Missal containing St. Ildefonso's De Per-
petua Virginitate, and various parts of the
Mass.

Written on vellum. The handwriting and illuminations
appear to belong to the Xth or XIth century. It consists
of 122 leaves, measuring 30ᶜᵗˢ· by 25ᶜᵗˢ·.

Fig. 1.

There is an index at the beginning, which was probably written by *Manuel Salazar*, a scribe of choir-books. It is stated therein that this volume is one of the most remarkable MSS. which exist at the Cathedral of Toledo. The tradition there was that the masses this volume contained were composed by St. Ildefonso (A.D. 606–668). Cath. Toledo, 35, 7.

II.

Codex containing a Gothic Missal with the Offices and Masses from the last prayer of matins of the first Sunday in Lent until the second vespers of the third day of the Easter festivities.

The Lamentations of Jeremias are at the end. This volume is written on vellum in writing of the Xth to the XIth century. It consists of 194 leaves, measuring 30$^{cts.}$ by 25$^{cts.}$. Cath. Toledo, 35, 5.

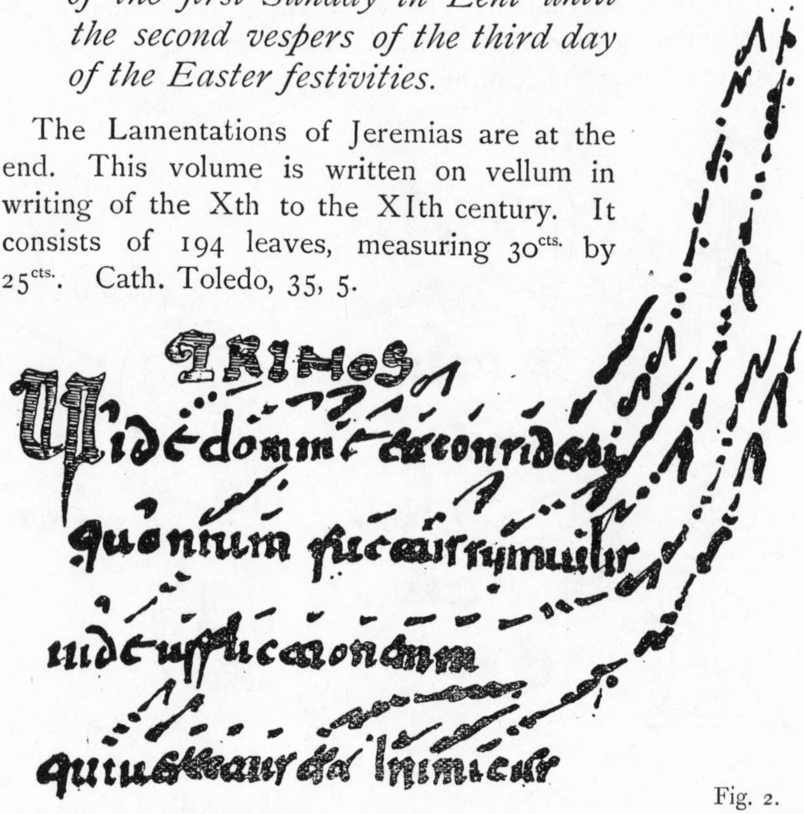

Fig. 2.

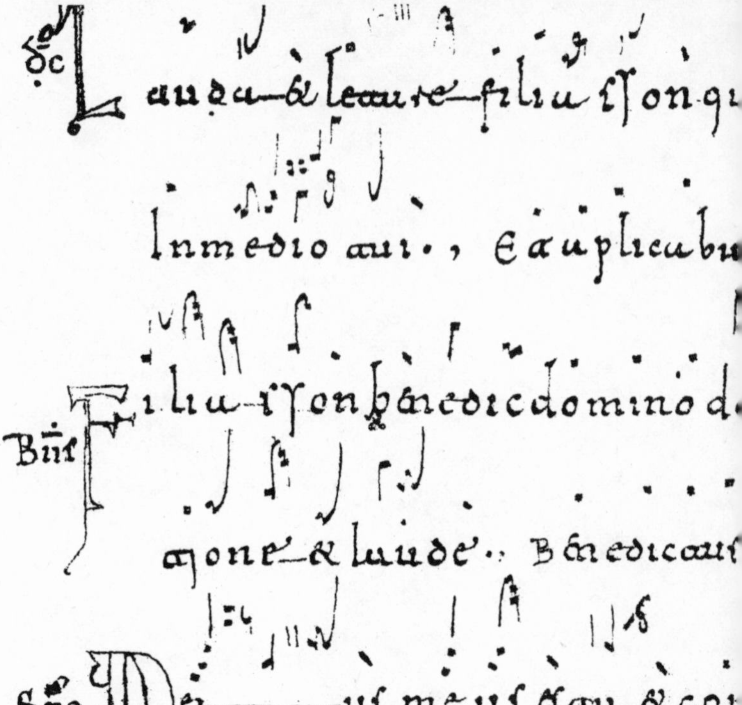

Sc Lauda a[n]i[m]a mea filiu[m] e[s]on qu

In medio au[t]. . , et a[m]plicabu

Bñ Filiu[m] e[s]on benedic domino d

a[ti]one et lau[n]de. . Benedicaus

Sño Deus me us e[s]au et co

us e[t] [s]au et [s]ulau bo a[t]

domine quoniam e[s]audi[t]

au[n]duce[t] dominum l[n]fun

ce ego ueniam & habitabo

elio In omni benedic

bor ab illa luia deus me

luiu. iii Confice bor ab

& fuccaus& mi ei In su luxe. alle.

Iusalle luiu. ii lle uiu.

alle luiu utta.

III.

Muzarabic Breviary.

Written on vellum in handwriting of the Xth or XIth century. It consists of 230 leaves, measuring 39$^{cts.}$ by 28$^{cts.}$. The beginning and end are missing, and it is badly mutilated in the middle. On the leaves, which are left in good condition, there is a great quantity of music written with Visigothic annotation. It belonged to the monastery of San Millan in la Rioja. Bibl. de la Real Academia de la Historia, F, 190.   Fig. 3.

IV.

Muzarabic Breviary.

Written on vellum in writing of the Xth or XIth century. It consists of 174 leaves, measuring 33$^{cts.}$ by 26$^{cts.}$ It

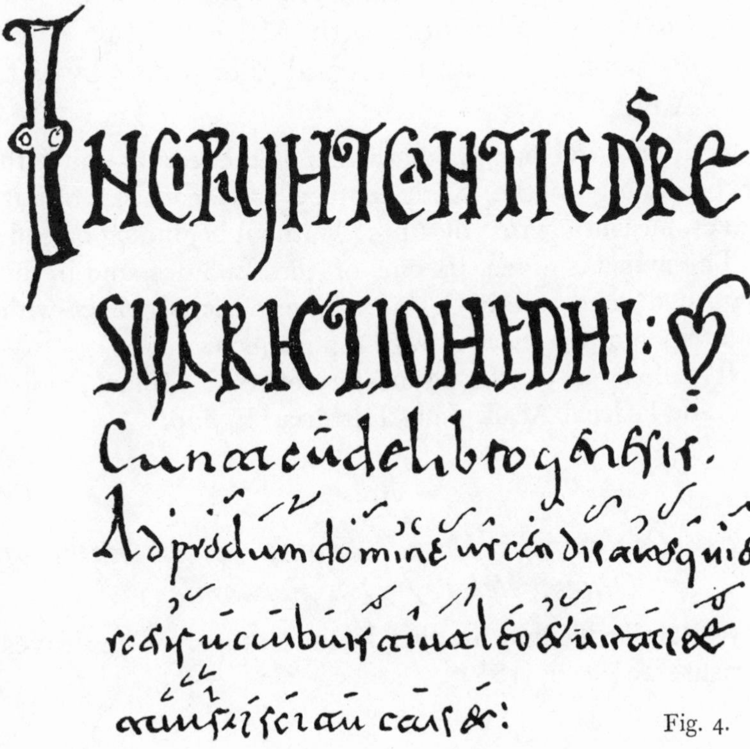

Fig. 4.

contains Psalms, Chants, and Hymns, and a great quantity of music written with Visigothic notes. Some of the music has been erased.

On two capital letters on p. 150 may be read *Abundantius presbiter librum.* The end is missing.

A brief description of this MS. and a photographic facsimile appeared in *Exempla scripturae visigoticae.* Ewald and G. Loewe, Heidelberg, 1883, fol. 27. Formerly at the Cathedral of Toledo ; now Bib. Nac. de Madrid, C, 35, 1.

v.

Codex, which contains De Reprimenda Avaritia; De Perfecta Concordia; De Abstinentia Occultanda ; the office of Litanies with its Music : *Passio Beatissimorum Martyrum Cosme et Damian,* with Music; the *Book of Sentences,* and several Sermons by St. Augustin.

Written on vellum, in characters of the end of the Xth or beginning of the XIth century. It consists of 95 leaves, measuring 19$^{cts.}$ by 14$^{cts.}$. Without beginning or end.

The music is given in one of the Litanies, and in the mass dedicated to San Cosme. The music is written with dots upon a line marked with a puncheon.

It belonged to the Monastery of San Millan, Rioja. Bibl. de la Real Acad. de la Historia, F, 228.

VI.

Liber Psalmorum David, known by the name of " Diurno del rey Don Fernando 1°."

Written on vellum in the XIth century. The leaves measure 29$\frac{1}{2}$$^{cts.}$ by 18$\frac{1}{2}$$^{cts.}$.

It contains the Calendar, the Psalms, and several Nocturns and Responsories. The music is given on the responsories ; it is written without lines and in dots in some instances on the text on a red line.

On the page before the nocturns and responsories, appears the name of the artist and scribe who illustrated this MS.

> " Era millena novies
> Dena quoque terna
> Petrus erat Scriptor
> Frictosus deniq. pictor."

This date corresponds to era 1098, A.D. 1055. Bibl. of the University of Santiago de Galicia.

VII.

Gothic Manual.

Written on vellum in the XIth century. It consists of 173 leaves, measuring $21\frac{1}{2}^{cts.}$ by 14^{cts}. It begins in this manner :—

" In nomine domini noster iesu christi incipit liber canticorum de toto circulo anni era millesima nonagesima septima :" this corresponds to A.D. 1059. The date and author's name is repeated at the end : " Explicit liber canticorum et orarum deo gratias. Amen. In XVII° Kalendas Junias era MXLVII[a] christoforus indignus scripsit mementote."

It contains music written with Visigothic signs.

A slight description of this MS. is given in " Exempla Scripturae Visigoticae," by P. Ewald and G. Loewe, Heidelberg, 1883. Fol. Tab. XXXII.

King's Library, Madrid, 2, 7, 5.

Fig. 5, p. 28.

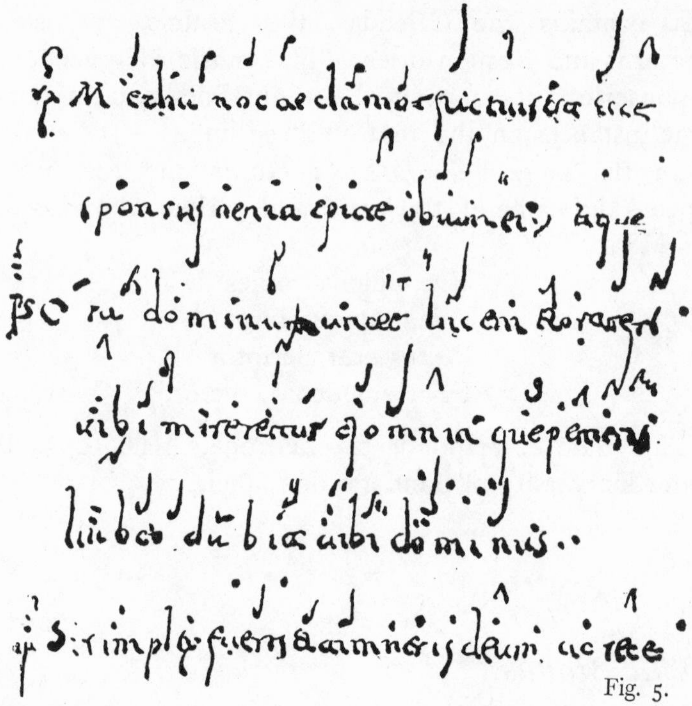

Fig. 5.

VIII.

Antiphonary of King Wamba.

Written on vellum in the XIth century. It contains 200 unfoliated leaves, measuring 33$^{cts.}$ by 24$\frac{1}{2}$$^{cts.}$. It contains ecclesiastical Rituals, Masses, Antiphons and various chapters written on different subjects ; among them there are some in which instructions are given to sing with proper devotion. " Incipit prefacio libri Antiphon sub metro heroicum elegiacum dictato." " Admonitio Cantoris sub metro heroico et elegiacum dictatum, qualiter letiferam pestem vane glorie refugiat, et cor mundum labiaque in Deum canendo exhibeat."

This MS. has several interesting specimens of music with Visigothic notes.

Fig. 6.

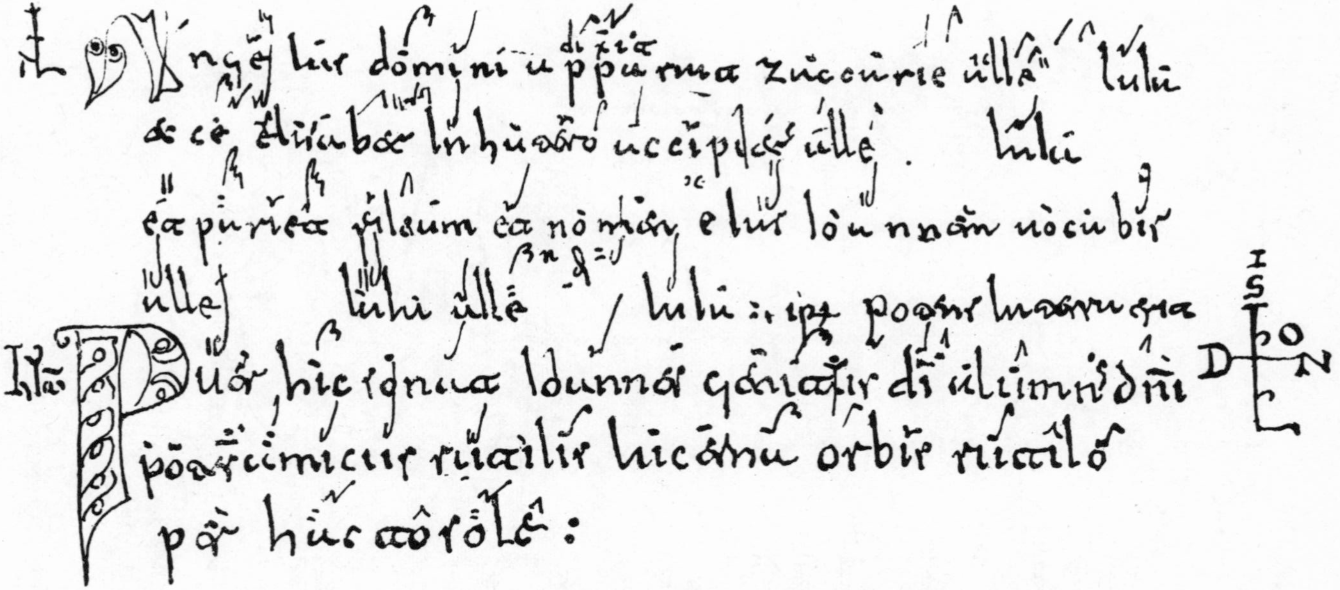

Fig. 7.

Several authors have thought that this volume was written during the reign of King Wamba (VIth century), but it must have been the copy of one which belonged to this period. There is a memorandum at the end in which it is stated that it was written by one named Arias in the era 1107, which corresponds to A.D. 1069. Archives of Cathedral of Leon.

71.   Fig. 6.

IX.

Codex containing the Gothic Missal, the Dominicas after Easter, and some Offices of the Saints.

The volume consists of 199 leaves, measuring $31^{cts.}$ by $20^{cts.}$ It is written on vellum in handwriting of the XIth century, and contains Visigothic musical annotation. The beginning and end are missing.

The musical notes have been omitted from several of the leaves. Cath. Toledo, 35, 6.

72.   Fig. 7.

X.

Codex containing a Gothic Missal, and the Offices and Masses from Easter to the XX Dominica after Pentecost.

This volume is written on vellum in handwriting of the XIth century. It contains Visigothic musical annotation.

It consists of 177 leaves, measuring $34^{cts.}$ by $26^{cts.}$. At the beginning there is an Index which was made in 1775 by Manual de Salazar by order of Cardinal Lorenzana. Salazar was the scribe who wrote the choir-books at the Cathedral of Toledo.

It belonged in the first instance to the Muzarabic parish

of Santa Olalla at Toledo. It is at present in the Library
of the Cathedral at Toledo, 35, 4.   Fig. 8.

XI.

Muzarabic manual, containing Ceremonies of the Church and some Masses.

Written on vellum in the XIth century. No beginning
or end. Several leaves are wanting from the centre. It
consists of 155 leaves, measuring 24$^{cts.}$ by 16^{cts}

This codex contains a great quantity of music, written
without lines in the Visigothic or Muzarabic annotation.
The MS. is splendidly written, the music is as clear as if
it had been engraved.

Fourteen erasures of this Visigothic music appear in the
text in Responsories and Antiphons in pp. 24, 26, 28vo, 29,
30vo, 31, 32, 32vo, 33, 33vo, 34, 35, 36vo, 37, they have been
substituted by another annotation of points, written upon
one line. It is probable that these corrections were made
very soon after the MS. was written. It is calculated
that these erasures were made by the French friars of
Cister or Cluny, who came to Spain at that time ; they
probably did not understand, or rather were not familiar
with, Visigothic annotation.

It is interesting that an Antiphon exists with both
these annotations. " In pace in id ipsum ob dormiam et
requiescam quoniam tu domine singulariter in spe constitu
isti me." This Antiphon is to be met with in folio 29vo
with the Visigothic signs, and in folio 33vo with *neums*
of points. Vide facsimiles of both these examples, and
two entire leaves with text and music give an idea of
this most interesting MS.

It belonged to the Monastery of San Millan (Emilianus)
in the Prov. of Rioja. Now at the Bibl. de la Real
Acad. de la Historia, F, 224.   Figs. 9, 10.

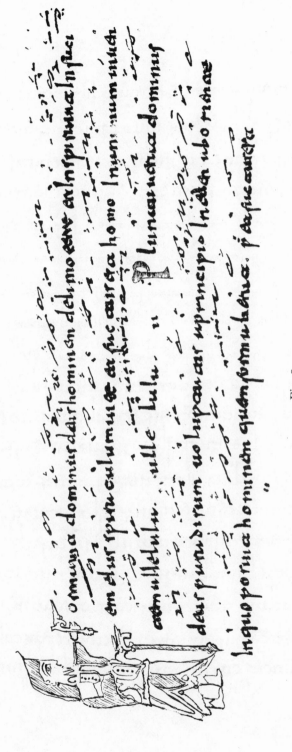

Fig. 8.

animam & corpus liberatum. hoc ipsius quod
corpus & hic depositum tibi conmendatur.
In pace ita ut abstrahe si nunc & ceptus.
perfruāinām paradisi letaq; um perfruat.

Laetit aiae clementiaqu divina uat sit aut͢ A In pace in idipsum
obdormium & requescā cǔm. quoniam tu domine singularit

In spe ————————— consta uisti me. P Porca mea dne usq; in finē.

Ora tē dnm. ut ad hoc tumuli notum tuis pangelum suum scm
sempr propiciuf uisitare digneatur. prsta.

neffabilis. dei paaris unigenitae filius. qui
humana tuatem nrē fragilitatis adsu
mēs. ideo In sepulcro requiescere passus est.
ut nos de sepulcris uitioru erigeres. et tua
tibi mēr resurrectionis. et ua sociares.
ad isto supplicationib; nris ea fube
uocatis humillimus. Quiam huncatu
mulum quem purificat et saluum
perud spassionē tuā salis ad recepta culū
fungat cutius. sū peccatuaub; benignissime.

scdm opscua aui. Leaifica dne animam
scua aui. Lclaifica dne finim auium.
neneminne̅ri ⁊ d̅s Iniquiaiaiaumeꝯ una
quarum: quan susciaiauia fuꝓr mali
desideri̅. Lice̅ enim peccuuia puarinꝰ
filium ꝫspm scm nonneꝫ auia sꝫ credi
dia ezelum dei habuia. ꝫdin quifaicia
omia udoruuia. pꝫrauiꝰ magna mꝫꝯꝫ

npace ꝉa depsuꝫdormiami ꝫtrequieꝫ cua quoniam audomine
singulariaꝫInspe coniacaui came. ⁊ Torromen dne.

nae ppe d̅s. quiꝭ puꝯ ungelorum eaꝫe
quiꝭ omnium elecaorum. clanaaꝫ
fucquꝯrum requiꝭ eꝫe finim auium.
Y a aenporeludiciaui susciaiauaū amor
ais. dormiaqone aucumse cꝫlꝫai lucꝉa
leaeauiꝭ uuiꝫe sine fine. ꝫeprꝫcaupꝫsumme

Aꝫpeciaꝫ aucdomuꝭ nuꝭ puradiꝭi Iunuara. uaaudillum
puaaium reuꝫaui ꝑiꝭ ubimoꝭ nonꝫꝭ ubidulceꝫquidium pꝫreupaa
ⱳ Dnꝭ regia ꝫaniul miei de ꝫaiꝭa: —— conloca uiꝭ. Vludulce

Fig. 10.

XII.

Liber Evangeliorum.

Written on vellum in the XIth century, finely ornamented with miniatures and letters painted in gold and colours.

It consists of 94 pages, measuring 27$^{cts.}$ by 16$^{cts.}$. Inside the binding are the following memorandums :—

",Codex MS. perantiquum magna cura pretioque maximo in urbis direptione redemptus S. Ecclesiae Toletanae dono datus a suo Praesule Card^{le} de Lorenzana.

" Hic codex redolet seculum X sive XI ; nulla etenim in hoc Evangeliario festivitas reperitur seculo XI posterior."

On several of the pages there are passages of music marked with points on a black line. Between these lines, which are marked with ink, three and four lines are sometimes marked with a puncheon, this generally occurs between the words of the chant. Bibl. Nac. de Madrid, Reservado, 6^{a}, 2.

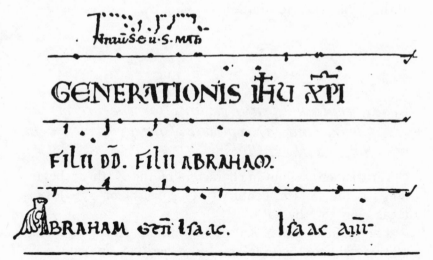

Fig. 11.

MANUSCRIPTS OF THE XITH or XIITH CENTURY.

I.

Codex containing a Breviary for the use of the Choir, with the Liturgy in Solfa written without lines.

This volume is written on vellum in characters of the end of the XIth or beginning of the XIIth century. It consists of 176 leaves, measuring 38$^{cts.}$ by 24$^{cts.}$.

There is an Index at the beginning written on vellum, apparently in the XVIIIth century.

It belonged to the Cathedral of Toledo, and is at present in the Bibl. Nac. de Madrid, 44, G, s.   Fig. 12.

II.

Codex containing a Breviary for the use of the Choir, and a complete Liturgy written in Solfa without lines.

Written on vellum in characters of the XIth or beginning of the XIIth century. It consists of 176 leaves measuring 38$^{cts.}$ by 24$^{cts.}$.

The whole of this MS. contains music. At the beginning of the volume there is an Index written on vellum in the XVIIIth century. Cath. Toledo, 44, 1.

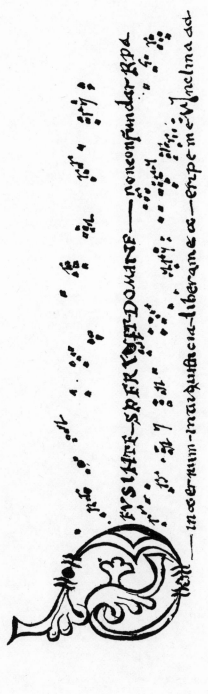

Fig. 12.

Fig. 13.

III.

A splendid Codex very richly ornamented, pro-
bably in the XIth or XIIth Century. It
contains the Antiphonary and Roman Re-
sponses written in ancient Solfa.

The whole of the volume contains musical notes written
upon a single line. The other lines are marked with a
puncheon. Two leaves have been added in the middle of
the MS. at a later period. The vellum is painted red,
and the handwriting is different in colour; the music is
already written on a tetragram of coloured lines, with
neums and points denoting the period of transition in
musical writing. The volume consists of 302 leaves,
measuring 43$^{cts.}$ by 31$^{cts.}$. Twelve or fourteen leaves have
been torn out of the volume.

It belonged to Cardinal Zelada; it is at present in the
Cath. Toledo, 48, 14.

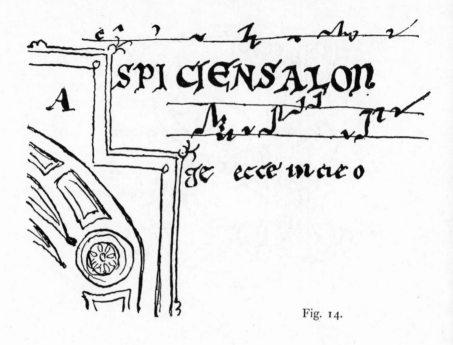

Fig. 14.

IV.

Choir Book.

Written on vellum in handwriting of the end of the XIth to beginning of the XIIth century. It consists of 189 leaves, measuring 27$^{cts.}$ by 17$^{cts.}$. The beginning and end are wanting.

Several of the fine miniatures have been coarsely torn out of the volume; only one remains complete, which represents our Lord inside the *vesica piscis*.

The music is on a line marked with a puncheon, with points in the French manner of the time. It contains a number of varieties of Glorias and Antiphons.

This MS. belonged to the Monastery of San Millan. Bibl. de la Real Academia de la Historia, F. 219.

V.

Commentary on the Apocalypse and St. Jerome's Treatise on the Book of the Prophet Daniel.

Written on vellum in characters of the end of the XIth and beginning of the XIIth century. It consists of 269 leaves, measuring 38^cts. by 23^cts..

This volume is at the British Museum; it is described in "Paleographia Sacra Pictoria" by J. O. Westwood, London, 1855. "The first leaf," says Mr. Westwood, "is extraneous, being evidently taken from a coëval choral book, the lines being marked with musical notes." He gives a specimen of the music, which belongs undoubtedly to the Visigothic period.

Mr. Westwood's remarks on the MSS. written in Spain in the Visigothic character are highly interesting. British Museum, Add. MS. 11, 695.

VI.

Gothic Codex, which comprises:

The office of St. Martin, with an account of his life written by Severus Sulpicius; the office of St. Millan; the office of the Assumption of the B. Virgin, with chants

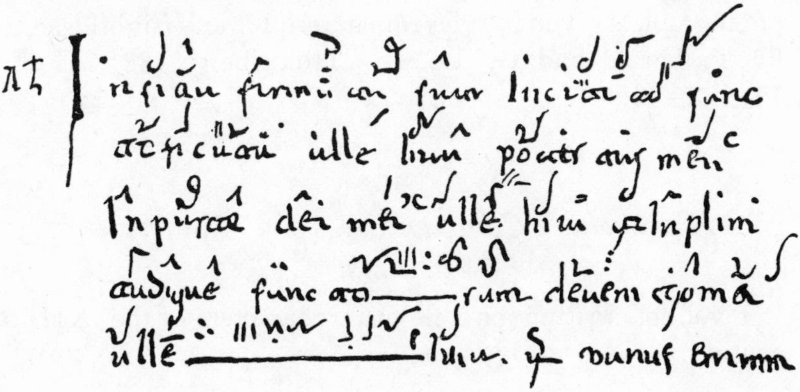

Fig. 15.

and musical notes; and the life of St. Millan (Emilianus) written by St. Braulio.

1 vol. 8vo. illuminated in colours on vellum in the XIIth century, consisting of 99 leaves. Cath. Toledo, 33, 2.

VII.

Gothic Breviary, containing the office of Lent according to the Muzarabic Ritual.

Written on vellum with black and red ink, measuring $27\frac{1}{2}^{\text{cts.}}$ by $19\frac{1}{2}^{\text{cts.}}$.

It contains 122 leaves, and was probably written in the XIIth century. It is not illuminated, but is full of musical notes. It belonged to the parish of Santa Justa y Rufina of Toledo, from whence it was taken to the Cathedral. At present this Breviary is at the Bibl. Nac. Madrid, 35, 2.

At the end :—" Finit. Deo gratias. hic liber per manus Ferdinandum Joannes presbiter ecclesiae sanctarum Justae et Ruffinae civitatis Toleti in mense Aprilis. Offeratur quiquis legerit. Ora pro me. Emenda eum prudenter et noli me maledicere si Dñum nostrum Jesum Christum abeas protectorem."

A slight description of this codex and a facsimile in photograph is given in " Exempla Scripturae Visigothicae," by P. Ewald and G. Loewe, Heidelberg, 1883. Fol. Plate XXX.   Fig. 16.

VIII.

St. Augustin. Commentaries on the first fifty Psalms.

1 vol. fol. written on vellum in characters of the XIIth century.

It formerly belonged to the Library of the Cathedral of Toledo, and is at present in the Bibl. Nac. Madrid, 14, 1.

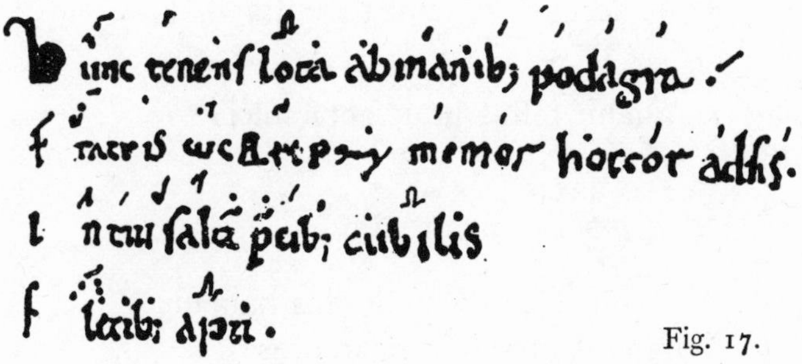

Fig. 17.

This volume also contains the following composition in Sapphic and Adonic verses written by a friar who appears to have been called Osbertu. The stanzas are full of musical notes.

Metrŭ Saphicvm : constans ex trocheo . spondeo . dactilo ultimus indifferenter ponitur quod quidam cecinit in hylaritate sue infra portas filie Syon coram.

> Dum cibis corpus modicus fouetur
> Pinguis aruina stomacus macrescit !
> Dum ne non pinsat puteal palati
> Crapula putris !

> Cordis ignescat generosus ardor.
> Mentis excrescat pia fortitudo
> Longuis prisca tetrici fugata
> Criminis obba :

Mittis ut frondes zephirus uirentes

veris accessu reuehit tepentis

seu uelut tellus liquefacta sulcis

Signit orexim

Mollibus sic nos moderans habenis
Suggerat uires uitio carentes
Dedat et fletus nimios ocellis
Spiritus almus :

Hoc Agustini studiu uolum̃ !

Dum ego rudis normæ modulis docerer.

Tum pia frates Aderaldus abbas

Lege regebat :

Ac regat glisco diuturnus æuo
Dis mori proquo paterer libenter
Si ut undenos sibi lucis auctor
adderet annos :

Cui Deus fidum sotians alumnum
Quem pię sorti coniuet priorem
Corrigens segnes · pietate mittes
Temperat omnes :

Qualis auroræ rutilans ab ortu
Phebus albescit radio micanti :
Noctis incusas spetiosus alas
      Rumpere curat :

Talis est huius penetrat libelli
Intus augustum recreans ocellum
Luminis pulpæ scabiem fugantis
      Dote salubri :

Fletibus largis auet immolari
Intimum cuius liber hic uibrauit
Sepia nexus habiles notaui
      Sirmatis ampli :

Hunc tenens loca ab manibus podagra
Fratris ωCℜℋℙℷ memor hortor adsis
Intui saltim precibus cubilis
      Flectibus apti.

Vt dei cernas sabaoth tribunal
Cœtibus sacre mercar iungi
Cum quibus possis pie dytirambi
    . . . . atis uti . amen.

IX.

Roman Missal.

Written on vellum in writing of the XIIth century. It consists of 364 leaves, measuring 37$^{cts.}$ by 25$^{cts.}$. The beginning and end are missing, some of the leaves are in bad condition.

This MS. has a great quantity of music written on a line marked with a puncheon, the words are separated by red lines.

It belonged to the Monastery of San Millan, Rioja. Bibl. de la Real. Acad. de la Historia, F, 185.

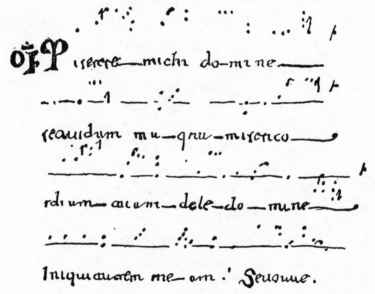

Fig. 18.

x.

Breviarium antiquissimum cum cantu Scripturæ iuxta methodum Gregorianum modulatæ, sed absque lineis.

Two volumes written on vellum in writing of the XIIth century. The beginning and end of both volumes are missing. The first contains 171 leaves, and the second 99, measuring 24$^{cts.}$ by 16$^{cts.}$

The musical notes are written on a line marked with a puncheon. Bibl. del Escorial, iij, L, 3, 4.

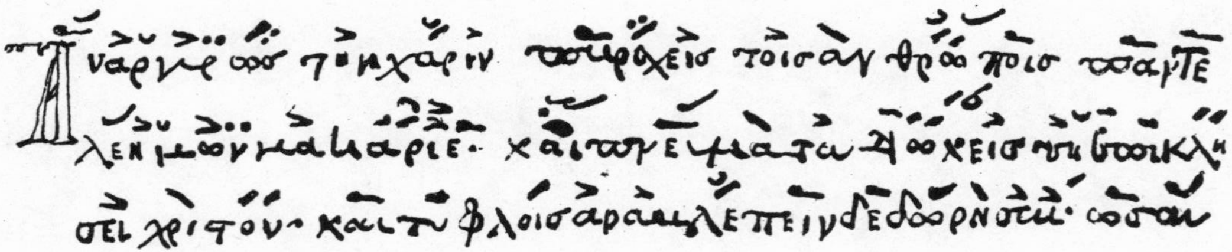

Fig. 19.

XI.

Codex containing a Greek Breviary of the Feasts of the Summer Months of the Year.

It is written on vellum in handwriting which appears to be of the XIIth century, and contains 222 leaves, measuring 24$^{cts.}$ by 18$^{cts.}$.

This Codex belonged to Cardinal Zelada; afterwards it passed to the Cathedral of Toledo; at present it is in the Bibl. Nac. de Madrid, 31, 28.

Fig. 19.

XII.

Al Farabi. Elements of the Art of Music, اسطقسات في صناعة الموسيقي *by Abu Nazar Mohammed ben Mohammed ben Tarjan Alfarabi.*

Written on paper. It contains 91 leaves, measuring 20$^{cts.}$ by 14$^{cts.}$ 22 lines per page. Written in Arab *neski* letters which are rather larger in the titles than the text. Annotations on the margin written in Arabic in different handwritings. On several of the pages there are drawings of musical instruments, and figures with annotations in numbers and letters. The first folio and some of the others are in bad condition.

Al Farabi in this book studies the elements of music, the composition of different voices and musical instruments, and the different styles of harmonic compositions and musical annotations. This Codex is divided in parts [فن] and these in chapters [مقالة] ending with part iii.

In the first folio the title of the book is given كتاب موسيقي

" Book on Music," " Libro de Musica." The same given by Casiri in the list he gives of the works of this author.

Alfarabi was a Turk; he died A.D. 951 to 955. The following authors have written his biography :—Aben Halican, " Trans. Slane," vol. iii. p. 307, idem, text of Wüstenfeld, num. v. 17 ; Rossi, " Diz. Historico," p. 71 ; Casiri, " Bibl. Arabica Escurialense," p. 190 ; Wüstenfeld, "Geschichte der Arabischen Aertze," p. 53 ; Munk, " Mé-langes " ; Andre's " Orig. e Progresso d'ogni Letterat," vol. vii.

The best description of this MS. will be found in T. P. N. Land, "Recherches sur l'Histoire de la Gamme arabe," Leyde, 1884.

Land describes the three Codes which are known written by Alfarabi which are at Milan, Leyden and Madrid ; he considers the one at Madrid the most important and finest of the three. This MS. has a note in which it is stated that it was copied for Aben Bachcha of Zaragoza in the XIIth century. Land publishes a plate of the musical instruments which are to be found in the Madrid MS. Bibl. Nac., G, g, 86.

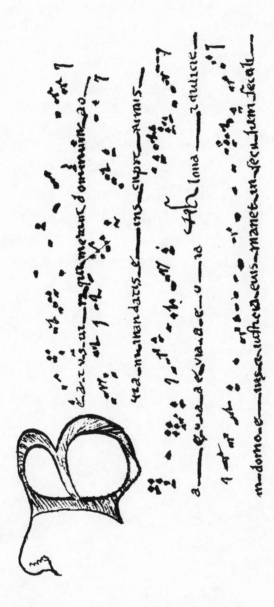

Fig. 20.

MANUSCRIPTS OF THE XIIITH CENTURY.

—◦—

I.

Codex which contains the Breviary adopted at Toledo after the Muzarabic Ritual was disused.

This volume is written on vellum in handwriting of the beginning of the XIIIth century. It consists of 143 leaves, measuring 24^{cts.} by 17^{cts.}. Cath. Toledo, 33, 5.

Fig. 20.

II.

Codex containing the Breviary which was adopted at Toledo after the Muzarabic Ritual had been abolished.

The Antiphones are written in Solfa for the use of the Choir. This MS. is of the XIIIth century, on vellum; the leaves measure 34^{cts.} by 26^{cts.}. It consists of 149 leaves. Written by different hands. Cath. Toledo, 35, 9.

Fig. 21 (see page 44).

III.

Codex containing a Breviary for the use of the Choir.

Written on vellum in the XIIIth century. It consists of 122 leaves, measuring 39½^{cts.} by 28^{cts.}. This MS. is in bad condition.

Fig. 22.

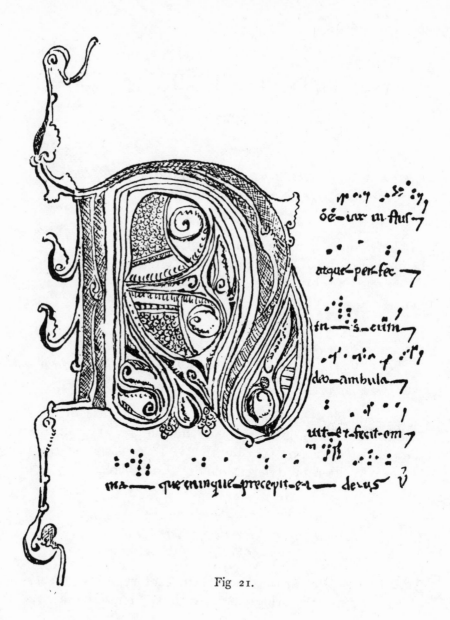

Fig 21.

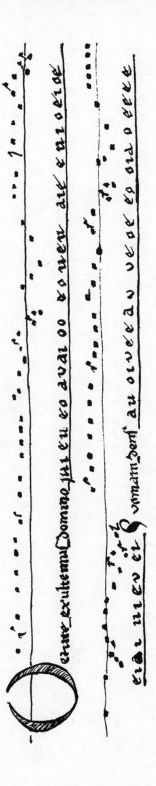

Fig. 22.

The music is on a single line marked with a puncheon. The *Invitatories* are written in a curious way, the vowels only are given; this manner was adapted afterwards. *Seculorum Amen.* Abbreviated into *Euouae.* Cath. Toledo, 44, 2.

IV.

Codex which contains Antiphons, Responses, and Lessons.

The music is on one line. The beginning and end of this MS. are missing. The neums are very legible. Written on vellum in the XIIIth century. It consists of 198 leaves, measuring 35^{cts.} by 25^{cts.}. It belonged to Cardinal Zelada, and passed after his death to the Cathedral of Toledo, 48, 15.

Fig. 23.

V.

Codex of a Roman Missal.

Written on vellum. The ornamentation and writing is of the end of the XIIth or beginning of the XIIIth century.

It consists of 150 leaves, measuring 35$^{cts.}$ by 26$^{cts.}$. The music is written on four lines; the lower one is marked with a puncheon, the second is painted red, it contains the key of Fa; the third is painted yellow, on this is the key of Do; the upper line is simply marked with a puncheon. Cath. Toledo, 39, 3.

Fig. 24.

VI.

Codex containing the Breviary which was adopted at Toledo after the Muzarabic Ritual was abolished.

Written on vellum in handwriting of the XIIIth century. It consists of 91 leaves, measuring 25$^{cts.}$ by 15$\frac{1}{2}$$^{cts.}$. Some are very much deteriorated. Cath. Toledo, 33, 4.

Fig. 25.

VII.

Codex containing Music, written in the XIIIth Century.

This volume contains chants for one, two, three and four voices. The five lines are used.

Written on vellum. It consists of 142 leaves, measuring 16$\frac{1}{2}$$^{cts.}$ by 11$\frac{1}{2}$$^{cts.}$.

This MS. is of the highest interest. Cath. Toledo, 33, 23.

Fig. 26.

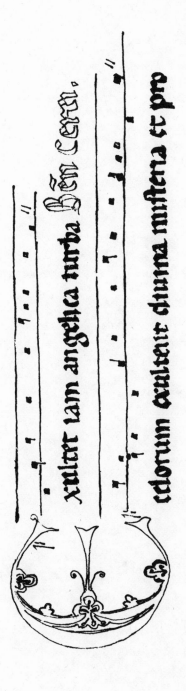

Fig. 24.

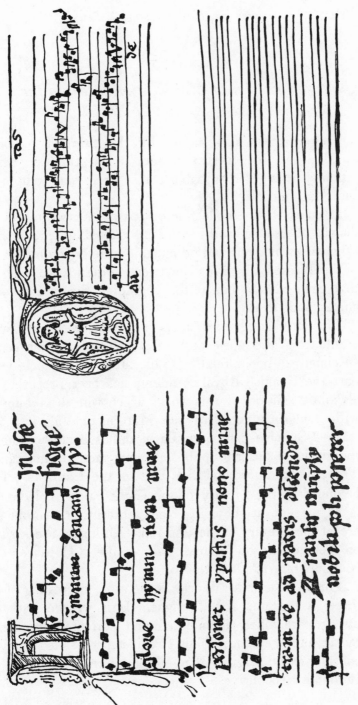

Fig. 25.

Fig. 26.

VIII.

Cantigas de Santa Maria, attributed to the King Don Alonso el Sabio.

This work is also known by the title of "Loores et Milagros de Nuestra Señora"; the tradition exists, although it is an improbable one, that it was written by the King himself.

It consists of a collection of 401 poems, written in the dialect of Galicia, and indifferent metres, upon miracles, sanctuaries, images, and other subjects referring to the life of the Blessed Virgin. They were written to be sung, so that each cantiga has at the beginning the music which corresponds to it.

This interesting work has never been published. Some facsimiles of the music and the poems have been given as specimens in books relating to literature. For some years past the Spanish Royal Academy has been preparing an elaborate edition of this work, which will shortly appear with numerous notes, by the Marquis of Valmar. The learned Spanish composer, Barbieri, has been working at the music in order to publish it with modern annotation. Three most important MSS. exist of the Cantigas. One belonged to the Library of the Cathedral of Toledo, and is at present at the Bib. Nac., Madrid; the other two are at the Library of the Escorial. All three are written on vellum in the second half of the XIIIth century, contemporary to Don Alonso.

This MS., now at Madrid, is the most interesting of the three, it contains 100 Cantigas. It is written with the utmost care, finely illuminated and corrected apparently by the author's hand. This circumstance has led many to consider it the original MS. It measures $31^{cts.}$ by $21\frac{1}{2}^{cts.}$. It contains 160 leaves.

on Affonſo de Caſtela
de Toledo de Leon
Rey: e ben des Compoſtela
ta o Reyno Daragon
de Cordoua. de Jahen
de Seuilla outroſſy
e de Murça u gran ben
lhs fez deus com aprimor
de Algarue que gãou
de mouros e noſſa fe
metteu y. e as poblou
Badallouz q̃ Reyno e
uit antigue que tolleu
a mouros Neule Xerez
Beger Medina prendeu
e Alcala outra uez.
que des Romãos Rey
e per dereit e Sennor
eſte Liuro com acher
fez. a onrre a Loor
da uirgen ſanta maria
que eſte madre de deus
en que ele muyto fia.
Poren dos miragres ſeu
fezo cantares e ſões
ſaboroſos de cantar
todos de ſennas razões
com q̃ poddes achar.

Eſta ea primeira cantiga de loor de
ſanta maria ementando os VII. goyos
que ouue de ſeu fillo.

deſoge mais q̃r eu
trobar. pola ſeñor
õrrada.. enq̃ deg q̃ſ carne fillar beeita
e ſagrada. por nos dar gran ſoldada.
no ſeu Reyno e nos herdar. por ſeg
de ſa maſnada. de uida p̃lõgada. ſen

Fig. 27.

The two MSS. at the Library of the Escorial contain many more compositions, and are far more richly illuminated. The one at this Library (j, T, 1) consists of 256 leaves, measuring 48½$^{cts.}$ by 33$^{cts.}$. It contains 292 Cantigas, with a number of fine miniatures which represent the events related in the poems. They contain numerous most interesting archæological and artistic details, arms, costumes, buildings, and music. The number of miniatures and ornamented letters amount to 1,292.

The second MS. of the Cantigas at the Library of the Escorial (j. 6, 2) consists of 361 leaves, measuring 40½$^{cts.}$ by 27½$^{cts.}$. It contains 401 Cantigas. It is not as finely decorated as the former one, but many of the miniatures are beautiful. The music is placed at the beginning of each of the songs. It is the most complete of the three. The name of the scribe, Juan Gonzalez, appears in the last composition.

The music is written in square notes on five lines; these are sometimes black, and at times there are four, three, two, or one which are painted red, and the series of vignettes or drawings representing fifty-one musicians of the XIIIth century, each one playing a different instrument. It is the most complete representation known of Spanish music and musicians of the time; these miniatures have been published by Señor Aznar in his interesting work, "Indumentaria Española."

Philip II. took these two MSS. to the Library of the Escorial from the Cathedral of Seville, where they had been bequeathed by Don Alfonso himself. (*See* facsimile of the first page of MS. j. 6, 2, and in Appendix the figures of musicians.)

IX.

Missae Manuale cum Notis Musicalibus.

Written on vellum in handwriting of the XIIIth century. It consists of 37 leaves, measuring 16$^{cts.}$ by 9$^{cts.}$. Without

beginning or end.   It contains music written in small
square points on a red line.   Bibl. Nac. de Madrid,
C, 145.

x.

Liber Cantus Chori.

MS. written on vellum in the XIIIth century.   It consists of 116 leaves, measuring 27$^{cts.}$ by 17$^{cts.}$ and musical
compositions for two voices.   The neums appear without
coloured lines ; there are traces of tetragrams marked
with a compass.   Bibl. de Don F. A. Barbieri.

MANUSCRIPTS OF THE XIVTH CENTURY.

I.

Codex which contains an Antiphonary of the Sundays and Feasts for the Year.

The volume is written on vellum, probably in the XIVth century. It consists of 153 leaves, measuring 27^{cts.} by 17^{cts.}. The whole of the MS. is full of music, which is written on four lines, one of which is painted red. This line varies sometimes in its position.

This MS. is highly interesting, it belonged to Cardinal Zelada. It is at present in the Cathedral of Toledo, 33, 24. (Fig. 28, p. 52.)

II.

Ancient Evangelistary according to the Missal of Toledo.

Written on vellum in character of the XIVth century. It contains 165 leaves, measuring 26^{cts.} by 17^{cts.}. Finely illuminated in gold and colours.

The music is written on a single line, which appears to have been marked with lead. In several pages the musical notes have been left out, although the places have been marked by the scribe who wrote the text. Cath. Toledo, 35, 19. (Fig. 29, p. 53.)

Fig. 28.

Fig. 29.

III.

Ritual of the Congregation of Perugia.

Written on vellum in handwriting of the XIVth century. It contains 81 leaves, which measure 24$^{cts.}$ by 16$^{cts.}$.

The music is written on two lines, painted yellow and red. The key of Fa is on the red line, on the yellow line the key of Do; they are not always together. Cath. Toledo, 39, 20.

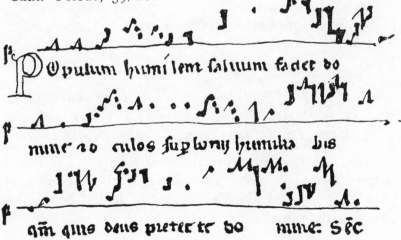

Fig. 30.

IV.

Roman Missal.

Written on vellum in handwriting of the XIVth century. The volume consists of 370 leaves, measuring 38$^{cts.}$ by 25$^{cts.}$. Some of the leaves are in bad condition.

This MS. is full of musical notes, written upon three and four lines. The key of Fa (F) is written on the red, the key of Do on the yellow line. On some of the pages there is only a red, on others only a yellow line. The remaining lines are marked with a puncheon. In one instance the music is written on four lines which have been marked with lead.

This codex is especially interesting owing to the beautiful manner in which the music is written. Cath. Toledo, 52, 11. (Fig. 31.)

V.

Missal for the use of the Choir, beginning with the Feast of the Nativity.

This volume is written on vellum in characters of the early part of the XIVth century. It is full of music written on a line marked with a puncheon. It consists of 148 leaves, measuring 33$^{cts.}$ by 24$^{cts.}$. Cath. Toledo, 35, 10. (Fig. 32.)

VI.

Missal, or fragment of a Missal of the Liturgy of Toledo, containing the Preparation for the Mass, the Ordinary, and Collects for the year.

This MS. is very finely written on vellum. The Initial letters are splendid. The study of the Calendar of Toledo, compared with the Feasts in this Missal, prove it was written from 1302 to 1369.

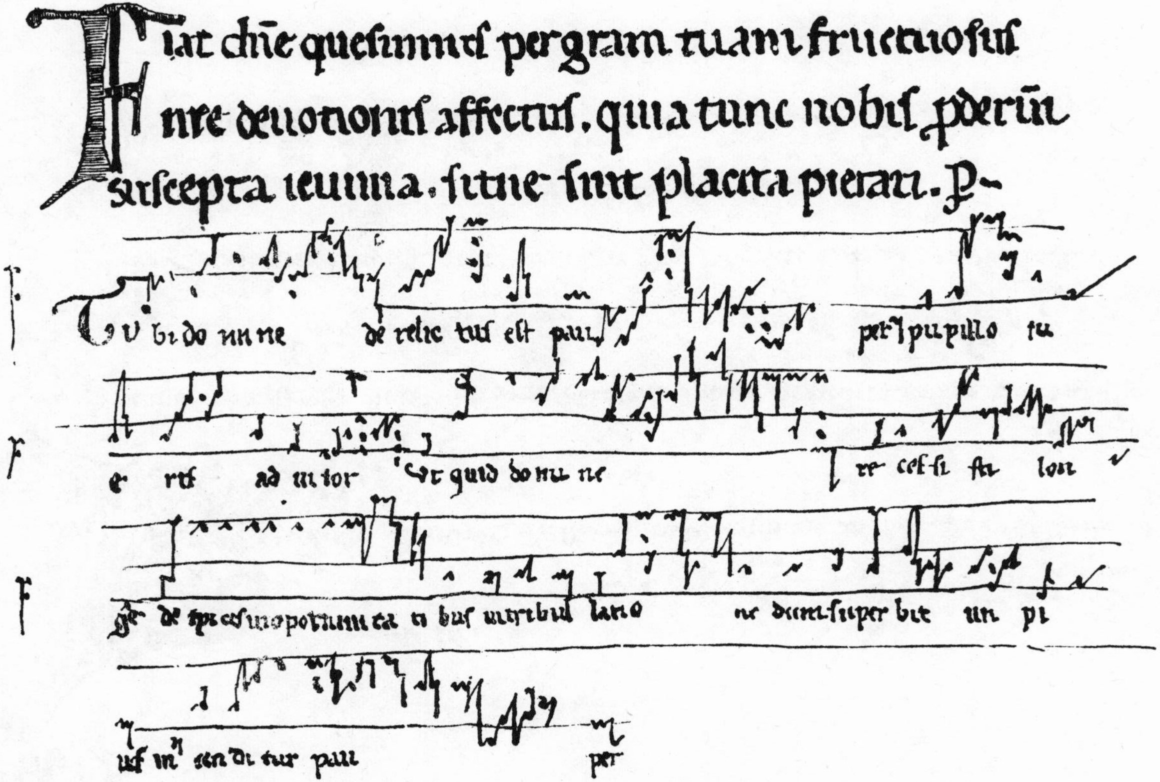
Fiat dñe quesumus per gratiam tuam fructuosus
nostre devotionis affectus. quia tunc nobis proderunt
suscepta ieiunia. si tibi sint placita pietati. P-

Fig 31.

Fig. 32.

The volume consists of 55 leaves, measuring 36$^{cts.}$ by 25$^{cts.}$. The musical notes are placed on four lines, with one exception as given below, which occurs at the end of the MS. in which the Pentegram is given. Cath. Toledo, 35, 11.

VII.

Codex which contains fragments of Breviaries and Roman Missals with Prefaces in Solfa.

A splendid MS. written on vellum, with gold and finely-coloured letters in characters of the XIVth century. It consists of 172 leaves, measuring 23$\frac{1}{2}$$^{cts.}$ by 15$^{cts.}$.

The title is " Prefaciones et Oraciones."

It belonged to Cardinal Zelada; it is at present in the Library of the Cathedral of Toledo, 37, 13. (Fig. 33, p. 56.)

VIII.

Codex which contains the Breviary with the Antiphons, and the Responsories set to Music.

The volume consists of 105 leaves, measuring 32$^{cts.}$ by 23$^{cts.}$. It is written on vellum in handwriting of the XIVth century.

The music is written upon four lines; three of them are marked with a puncheon; the fourth is painted red. The red line is generally at the bottom of the others; the

Fig. 33.

Fig. 34.

key of Fa (F) is always marked above it. The key of
Do (C) is in some instances marked upon one of the lines
which are punched. Some flats and quadrates are to be
met with among the musical notes.

This Codex belonged to Cardinal Zelada; it is at
present in the Library of the Cathedral of Toledo,
44, 3. (Fig. 34, p. 56.)

IX.

Ordinary of the Mass, with Prayers, Gospels, and Prefaces in Solfa.

Written on vellum in characters of the XIVth century.
It contains 69 leaves, measuring 20[cts.] by 15[cts.].

The music is written in two different ways; one on
three or four very fine indistinct lines which appear to
have been marked with a puncheon. On one of these

Fig. 35.

lines (the third or fourth) is generally marked the key of Fa. In the other the music is written on four or five lines, the third or fourth of these is a thick red line ; the others are very fine, black and indistinct. Cath. Toledo, 37, 12.

X.

Canon de Edificanda Ecclesia—
 Item. *Ordo Romanum qualiter agatur Concilium generale.* It. *Ordo qualiter Concilium agatur provinciale.* It. *Ordinatio de Solemnitate Coronationum Regis.* It. *De Significatione mystica Indumentorum pontificalium.*

Written on vellum in characters of the XIVth century. It contains 98 leaves, measuring 22$^{cts.}$ by 13$^{cts.}$. Some of the leaves measure 14$^{cts.}$ by 10$^{cts.}$.

The music is, in different parts of the MS., written upon four lines engraved with a puncheon.

It belonged to King Philip the Fifth's Private Library. Bibl. Nac. de Madrid, C, 82.

XI.

Liber Cantus Chori.

Written on vellum in characters of the XIVth century. It contains 240 leaves, measuring 17$^{cts.}$ by 10$^{cts.}$. The end is missing.

The whole MS. contains music, which is written on four lines marked with a puncheon.

It belonged formerly to the Private Library of King Philip the Fifth. Bibl. Nac. de Madrid, C, 132.

XII.

Liber Cantus Chori cum Notis Musicalibus.

Written on parchment in characters of the XIVth century. The end is incomplete. It consists of 156 leaves, measuring 15$^{cts.}$ by 9$^{cts.}$. The music is written upon four lines engraved with a puncheon.

It belonged to King Philip the Fifth's Private Library. Bibl. Nac. de Madrid, C, 153.

XIII.

Coeremoniale Romanum.

Written on vellum in characters of the XIVth century. It contains 157 leaves, measuring 21½$^{cts.}$ by 12$^{cts.}$.

The music is written on a red tetragram. Formerly in King Philip the Fifth's Private Library, now in the Bibl. Nac. de Madrid, C, 63.

XIV.

Cantoral Monastico.

Written on vellum in the XIVth century. It consists of 203 leaves. The music is written on a tetragram of red lines with square notes. This MS. is illuminated, the leaves measure 43$^{cts.}$ by 31$^{cts.}$. Bibl. de Don F. A. Barbieri.

XV.

Cantoral del Siglo XIV.

Written on vellum. The music is written on a tetragram with square notes, in some instances on a pentagram. It consists of 187 leaves, measuring 29$^{cts.}$ by 21$^{cts.}$. Bibl. de Don F. A. Barbieri.

XVI.

Missal, containing the Prefaces and some Masses dedicated to Our Lord, the B. Virgin, and Faithful departed.

Written on vellum in characters of the XIVth century, with finely-ornamented capital letters.

It consists of 117 leaves, measuring 36$^{cts.}$ by 27$^{cts.}$. Cath. Toledo, 35, 12.

XVII.

Ceremonial and Pontifical used at the Cathedral of Toledo.

This volume contains the Ceremonial used at the anointment and benediction of the King on his election by the clergy and the people. Bishops of different churches assisted at the ceremony. The ceremony used at the benediction of the Emperor follows this. The Bishops of Segovia and Palencia were present. The volume ends with the benediction for an Empress.

This Codex is probably the copy of an older one, probably of the Visigothic period.

It is written on vellum in characters of the XIVth century. It consists of 164 leaves, measuring 25$^{cts.}$ by 19$^{cts.}$. The whole of the music is written on a single line marked with lead. Cath. Toledo, 39, 12.

XVIII.

Ceremonial for the use of Bishops.

This volume is written on vellum in characters of the XIVth century. It consists of 129 leaves, measuring 29$^{cts.}$ by 19$^{cts.}$.

The musical notes are written on a single line marked with lead, without a key or colours. Cath. Toledo, 39, 14.

XIX.

Ceremonial and Manual for the use of Bishops. It contains the preparations for celebrating, and a formulary of solemn Benedictions for different Feasts of the Year.

This volume is written on vellum, in characters of the XIVth century. It consists of 65 leaves, measuring 25cts. by 19cts..

The musical notes are written on pentagrams marked with red lines. Cath. Toledo, 39, 13.

XX.

Roman Ceremonial.

Written on vellum in characters of the XIVth century. It contains 136 leaves, measuring 26cts. by 18cts..

The music is written on four, on three, and on two red lines; in some instances the music is incorrectly written. Cath. Toledo, 39, 17.

XXI.

Officium transfixionis, seu septem dolorum Beatissimae Virginis Mariæ ad missam, matutinum et utrumque vesperum. Item. *Officium sanctis Ivonis confessoris, Pauperum advocati.*

Written on vellum in writing of the XIVth century. It consists of 46 leaves, measuring 31cts. by 21cts..

The music is written on a red line. Bibl. del Escorial, ij. 6, 4.

XXII.

Cantoral de Dominicas y Ferias, with the Introits and Antiphons of the Offices of some Saints.

Written on vellum in writing of the XIVth century, except the last leaves, which are more modern in date.

It consists of 207 leaves, measuring $25\frac{1}{2}^{cts.}$ by $16\frac{1}{2}^{cts.}$.

The music is written sometimes on four, and sometimes on five red lines.

The title of this MS. is "Missale Cartusianum." Bibl. del Escorial, iij. I, 1.

XXIII.

Officivm praesentationis Bmae Virginis Mariae ex praecepto Sixti IV. Pontificis Maximi olim in Hispania celebrari solitum, valde tamen diversum ab hodierno hujus solemnitatis officio.

Written on vellum in characters of the end of the XIVth century. This MS. contains 26 leaves, measuring $46^{cts.}$ by $35^{cts.}$. At the back of the first leaf, "In festo presentationis virginis Marie ; quod festum, pmo fuit celebratum in francia : ad instanciam."

MANUSCRIPTS OF THE XVᵀᴴ CENTURY.

I.

Prefaces for different Feasts of the Year.

Written on vellum in characters of the XVth century. The music is at the end.   It contains 90 leaves, which measure 23ᶜᵗˢ· by 16ᶜᵗˢ·.   Cath. Toledo, 37, 14.

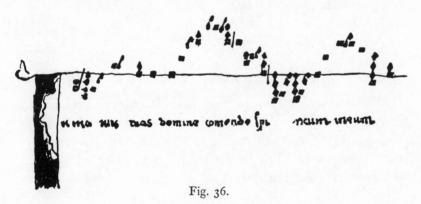

Fig. 36.

II.

Roman Missal.

Written on vellum, in handwriting of the XVth century.   It consists of 145 leaves, which measure 24ᶜᵗˢ· by 16ᶜᵗˢ·.   The music is on a red pentagram.   Cath. Toledo, 35, 18.

III.

Roman Ceremonial.

Written on parchment in characters of the XVth century. It contains 73 leaves, measuring $25^{cts.}$ by $19^{cts.}$. The music is written on two or three red lines.

This Codex has been added to in later times, for several passages appear to have been written in the XVIIth century. Cath. Toledo, 39, 18.

IV.

Psaltery, with Antiphonaries, Hymns, and Litanies.

Written on vellum in writing of the XIVth century. It contains 70 leaves, measuring $34^{cts.}$ by $24^{cts.}$. The music is written on three, or, in some instances, four red lines. Cath. Toledo, 60, 6.

V.

Missale mixtum secundum Ordinem Cartusiensem.

Written on vellum in the XVth century, illuminated in gold and colours. It consists of 6 leaves of calendar and 211 of text. The music is written with square notes on a tetragram. The leaves measure $32^{cts.}$ by $23^{cts.}$. Bibl. de Don. F. A. Barbieri.

VI.

Libro de Cantos.

Written on paper, 4to., written in the XVth century. It contains a number of *romances*, *villancicos*, and *letrillas*, with their music written on a pentagram. These compositions are by different authors; some of the names are given. It has no date. Bibl. Particular de S.M. el Rey. S. 2, Est. I. p. 5.

VII.

Missae Manuale cum Notis Musicalibus. Item. *Aliud sine Notis.*

Written on vellum in characters of the XVth century. In bad condition; the beginning is illegible and the end is missing.

These two MSS. contain 44 leaves: the first, measuring 16$^{cts.}$ by 9$^{cts.}$; the second, 18$^{cts.}$ by 13$^{cts.}$. The music is written on a red line.

Formerly in the Private Library of King Philip V, now in the Bibl. Nac. de Madrid, C, 145.

VIII.

Musica de Canto llano y de Organo.

Written on paper in writing of the XVth century. It consists of 50 leaves, measuring 20$\frac{1}{2}$$^{cts.}$ by 14$\frac{1}{2}$$^{cts.}$. The title-page is missing.

The music is written on a pentagram of red lines. The text is in Latin and Spanish. At the end it is stated that it was finished in Seville in 1480.

The author, in chapter I., speaks of the origin and cultivators of music from the earliest times. He names, among other musicians, Dustable, Dufay, Johannes Obeghem, master of the chapel of the King of France, Vinchois, Coustas, Willelmus Fanguens, and Johannes Martini. Bibl. del Escorial, c, iij, 23.

IX.

Roman Missal.

Written on vellum by Jacobelo de Capua, in 1483. The volume is full of fine illuminations painted in gold and colours. The music is written on a pentagram.

The MS. consists of 201 leaves, measuring 37^cts. by 27^cts.. It belonged to Cardinal Zelada, and is at present in the Cath. Toledo, 35, 17.

X.

Canto de Organo.

A volume in 4to, written on paper by different hands, at the end of the XVth century. It contains French, Italian, German, and Italian songs, and a few motets in Latin. The whole volume is written in music for three and four voices. This MS. begins with a list of the songs it contains. The musical hand follows, and a study in Latin of the manner of singing. Some of the names of the authors of the songs are legible. Among them appear Gay, Morton, Busnoie, or Busnois, Philipet de Pres, Georgius, Zuny, Agricola, and Caspae.

This volume consists of 181 leaves, badly foliated. Cath. Seville. Bibl. Colombina, Z, 135, 33.

XI.

Ordinarium Precum Ecclesiae Cathedralis Tolosanae, cum Hymnis et Antiphonis.

Written on vellum in characters of the XVth century. It contains 86 leaves, measuring 19^cts. by 11^cts.. This MS. is full of music written upon a single line marked with a puncheon.

It belonged to the private library of King Philip V. Bibl. Nac. de Madrid, C, 131.

XII.

A volume in 4to, which appears to have been written in Italy in the Fifteenth Century.

Part of it is written on vellum and the rest on paper; the handwritings are different. It contains the following tracts :—

1. "Ars Musicae mensurata" (Marchetti de Padua), "Lucidarium in Arte planae Musicae."

2. Marchetti de Padua, "Lucidarium in Arte planae Musicae."

3. Fr. Raymundus de Silva, "De Doctrina Finali fragmentum."

4. "Tractatus de Musica;" incerti authoris.

5. "Rationes Tonorum, secundum Boetium."

6. "De XIIII. Species Cantus; id est, quantae distantiæ possunt inveniri in Diapason."

7. "Ars, quomodo debet fieri Motteta."

8. "Regulae in discanta compositae per Fr. Nicolaum de Senis, Ordinis Servorum S. Mariae, et copiatae per Fr. Bernardum de S. Croce, Ord. Predicatorum, in Civitate Veronae."

9. Marchetti de Padua, "Super Cantum Planum."

Cath. Seville, Bibl. Colombina, Z, 135, 32. Variorum de Musica.

MANUSCRIPTS OF THE XVITH CENTURY.

I.

Roman Missal.

Written on vellum by Fr. Constancio de Monte Olivas in 1512. It is beautifully ornamented with colours and gold, the music on a red tetragram.

This MS. belonged to the Cathedral of Toledo. It is at present in the Bibl. Nac. de Madrid, 52, 6.

II.

Manual containing Instructions for the Administration of the Sacraments.

This volume consists of 38 leaves, measuring 21^cts. by 15^cts.. It is written on vellum in characters of the XVIth century. The musical notes are written on a red line. Cath. Toledo, 38, 24.

III.

Canciones Amorosas.

Written on paper, in writing of the XVIth century. It consists of 137 leaves, measuring 20^cts. by 14^cts..

It contains French and Italian songs. The music is on a pentagram of black lines.

This MS. belonged to Don Diego de Mendoza; his autograph is at the beginning of the volume. Bibl. del Escorial, iv, a, 24.

IV.

Missal belonging to Cardinal Ximenez de Cisneros.

This Missal consists of seven volumes written on vellum in the XVIth century. They compose a total of 1,543 leaves, measuring 46$^{cts.}$ by 33$^{cts.}$. The sixth and seventh volumes are 2$^{cts.}$ lower.

This Missal is most splendidly ornamented. The miniatures and initial letters are very fine. The music is written on a pentagram marked with red lines.

It belonged to the Cathedal of Toledo, and is now at the Bibl. Nac. de Madrid, 52, 16–22.

PRINTED WORKS ON THEORETICAL MUSIC.

I.

De Musica Practica. By Bartholomé Ramos de Pareja.

2 vols. in 4$^{to.}$. Bononie. 1482. Black letter.

Only one copy is known of this extremely rare work ; it exists in the Biblioteca del Liceo Rossini, dependent on the Municipality of Bologna.

The title-page of the first volume is missing; in its stead there is a leaf on which is written : "Librum istum prima pagina caret," &c. It does not contain any printed music, but several illustrations are to be found in the text. On p. 22 there is a red pentagram on which the music is written by hand. There are numerous manuscript notes on the margins which have been written by Gaffurio, Ramos de Pareja's enemy, who attacked his theory of "Temperamento," which was accepted in Europe at the end of a century. Gaffurio and Nicolas Borcio were its principal opponents. Borcio published a pamphlet entitled : "Adversus quemdam Hispanum veritatis praevaricatorem." At the end of the volume there is the following note : "Explicit musica practica Bartholomei Rami de Pareia Hispani et Betica provincia, Civitate Baeza, Gienii (Jaen) diocesi vel suffragane oriundi. Alme urbis Bononie dum eas ibidem publice lexeret. Impressa anno domini millesimo quatrigentesimo octuagesimo secundo quarto idus maii."

The second volume contains manuscript notes, but they are only to be found in the last leaves ; their author is not known. At the end is the following memorandum : " Explicit feliciter prima pars musice egregii famosi musici bartholomei parea hispan. dum publice musica bononie legeret in qua practica canto praecellit. Impressa vero ope industria ac expensis majus baltasaris de hiriberia anno domini m.cccclxxxii. die v junii."

These different dates have given rise to the supposition that the first edition was that of June 5. The following observations, taken from the Catalogue of the Bibl. dei Liceo Rossini must not be overlooked.

Note of the Catalogue on the first volume : " La diversita della presente edizione dall' altra del 5 Giugno che discrivesi nella scheda che a questa sussegue, consiste nell essere istampata la carta segnata 63 colla sua corrispondente insieme all' ultim a del libro, nel resto trovandosi i due esemplari della stessa stessisima edizione. In fatti nella stampa degli 11 di Maggio promette l'autore nel rectto dell' ultima carta di far succedere un altro volume a questo da lui pubblicato, la quel promessa non si vede nell esemplare col la data del 5 Giugno."

Memorandum contained in the second volume : " Qui deve aggiunguersi che nel presente esemplare non apaiano ristampate le tre carte suddette, ma bensi in quello colla data degli 11 Maggio giacche in esso e palese la diversita de caratteri che son piu grandi del resto del libro nelle tre carte ristampate : laddove la copia del 5 Giugno di cui ora parliamo ha una perfetta equaglianza di carattere in tutti : fogli del libro e quindi nelle tre memorate carte. Da cio si deduce che la copia del 5 Giugno ha tutti gl'indizj d'esser la stampa primitiva ed originale, e che o per errore o perche altro che noi non potremmo indovinare, fu posta la data anteriore dell' undici Maggio nell' esemplare che ha le tre carte ristampate."

At the Royal Library, Berlin, there is a MS. copy of Ramos de Pareja's work, written in the XVth century. It consists of 87 leaves in 4to. Sr Barbieri has made numerous extracts from this volume which are published in Sr Menendez Pelayos' " Hist. de las Ideas Esteticas en España," tom. ii. p. 660.

II.

⟨Incipiūt octo toni Artis Musice a patre sanctissimo gregorio ordinati 7 compositi qui quodam modo sunt claues Musice Artis.

At the end: " Esta obra fue emprimida en Seuilla por quatro alemanes compañeros. En el año de nuestro señor, 1, 4, 9, 2."

The book begins thus :

Fig. 37.

4to. Black letter. 7 unnumbered leaves, without text. This book treats of chant music ; the notes are excellently engraved, and the words printed. It appears to be the second part of a work written on chants. The title and name of the author are unknown. Bibl. de Toledo, 3^a, 2, 4.

Guillermi de Podio pre/sbyteri Commentariorum Mu/sices, ad reverendissimum il/lustrissimum-que Alphonsum de/Aragonia Episcopum Der/ tussensem. Incipit prologus.

Impressum in inclyta urbe Valentina Impensis | magnifici Jacobi de Villa: per Petrum Hagembach et Le | onardum Hutry alemanos. 1495. 68 leaves.

III.

❡*Esta es vna introduciō muy vtil : 7 breue de Canto llano, dirigida al muy magnifico señor dō Jua de fonseca obispo de Cordoua. Compuesta por el bachiller alonso spañon.*

At the end : ❡ " Vista 7 esaminada la presente obra: por el reuerēdo señor doctor herñado de la fuēte prouisor 7 veedor de las obras q̃ se īprimē en el arçobispado de Seuilla. ❡ Empremida por pedro brun. s."

4to.. Black letter. 12 unnumbered leaves, no title-page or title at the beginning. Bibl. de Toledo, 3ª, 2, 4.

A treatise on the theory of music, in which the elements of singing are explained with great minuteness. It is illustrated by numerous wood engravings.

This book must have been printed at the end of the XVth century, perhaps in the last year, the same in which Don Juan Rodriguez Fonseca was appointed Bishop of Cordova. The printer, Pedro Brun, was settled in Seville in 1492.

IV.

Lux Bella.

" Ars cantus plani cōposita breuissimo compendio lux bella nūcupata per baccalariū dominicū duranciū: 7 clarissimo dño petro ximenio curiensi episcopo reverendissimo : atq̃ sacratissime theologie peritissimo dedicata feliciter incipitur ad laudem dei."

4to. Black letter. 6 unnumbered leaves.

Written in Spanish, with some Latin words, wood engravings of music.

It ends : " Explicit lux bella : metrū 7 / mensura cantus plani."

This important and very rare book is supposed to have been printed at Salamanca at the end of the XVth century. Pedro Ximenes, to whom it is dedicated, was appointed Bishop of Coria in 1489.

The only copy known is at the Biblioteca de Toledo, 3ª, 2, 4.

Two other editions are known of Lux Bella, one " Sevilla por quatro alemanes 1492."

Sevilla, Jacobo Cronberger. 1518. 4to. Black letter.

v.

Sumula de Cāto / de Organo : Contrapunto y Com-po/sicion vocal y instrumental ; practica / y speculativa.

On the verso : " Siguese una sumula del canto de organo · contrapunto y cōposicion · vocal 7 instrumental con su theorica y practica. Cōpuesta por el bachiler [*sic*] domingo marcos duran fijo legitimo de juan marcos 7 isabel fernādez que ayan sancta gloria · cuya naturaleza es la noble villa que se dize de alconetar o de las garrouillas · va dirigida al reuerendissimo y muy magnifico señor don alfonso de fonseca arçobispo de Santiago mi señor." 4to. Black letter. 23 leaves. Bibl. de Toledo, 3ª, 2, 4.

A study of the theory and practice of music illustrated by numerous interesting examples of wood engravings. At the end there is a note, stating it was printed by order of Don Alfonso de Castilla, Rector of the studies of

Salamanca. This circumstance allows us to suppose that Archbishop Fonseca, to whom this work was dedicated, was a native of Salamanca. There are three Archbishops of Santiago who follow each other with the same name and surname; if so, he was Archbishop from 1463 to 1506, the date when this book was probably printed.

VI.

Ars magna. Deus cum tua summa perfectione. Incipit ars generalis ultima edita a magistro Raymundo lull.

Barchne impressum per Petrū posa completumq̄ Anno Domini M.D. primo decima mensis Aprilis dies Sabbato Santo | fuit opus istud.

Folio. Black letter. 92 leaves.

At the end there is a printed note in which it is stated that Lull wrote this book in 1308, shortly before his death.

There is a chapter which treats exclusively of music.

VII.

❡ Port⁹ : Musice correctus seu emendatus in quo nemo periclitabitur.

At the verso : " Ars cantus plani portus musice vocata siue organice cum proportionibus seu contrapunti cum duodecim gammis siue compositionis trium vel quattuor vocum cum intonationibus psalmorum officiorum seu responsoriorum aut manualis cum duabus figuris aspericis . seu lune aut mensium incipiendorum cum quattuor tpibus et nonis idibus et kalendis seu nuptiis celebrandis · que vela vocantur · composita per didacum a portu cantorem capellanum que collegii diui Bartholomei siti in nobili civitate Salamantina beneficiatum ecclesia sancte marie

oppidi de Laredo burgensis diocesis · correcta seu
emendata per reuerendissimum dominum Alfonsum de
castilia."

At the end : "Impressum fuit hoc opus salamantiae
pridie kalendas septembris . anno a natiuitate domini ·
m.cccccciiij."

4ᵗᵒ. Black letter. 12 unnumbered leaves, Latin text.
The marginal notes are in Spanish. Numerous examples
of wood engravings of chants, and organ music, counter-
point, and composition. This book is very rare and
very interesting. Bibl. de Toledo, 3ª, 2, 4.

VIII.

*Arte de Canto llano Lux videntis dicha. Copues/ta
por el egregio frey Bartholome de molina de
la ordē de los | minores: bachiller en sancta
theologia. Dirigida al muy reue/rendo y
magnifico señor don Pedro de ribera, obispo |
de Lugo, y por el dicho señor obispo aprovada.*

At the end : " Fue empremida la presente Arte en la
noble villa de Valladolid por Diego de Gumi. El a 25
dias del mes de Novembre ano del Señor de Mil
qniētos y vj. 4ᵗᵒ gotico. 12 leaves.

IX.

Comento sobre Lux Bella.

" Comiença una Glosa del Bachiller Domingo Marcos
Duran, fijo legitimo de Juan Marcos e Isabel Fernandez,
sobre el arte de Canto llano compuesta por el mesmo
llamada Lux Bella."

" Esta obra fue empremida en Salamanca a xvij de Junio

del año de nro señor de mill 7 quatrociētos y nouenta y
ocho años."

4ᵗᵒ·. Black letter. 38 unnumbered leaves. The title is
engraved on the first page. Biblioteca de Toledo, 3ª, 2, 4.

This work treats principally of the theory of vocal and
instrumental music, and is full of interesting details. A
number of contemporary authors are mentioned:—Juan de
Londres, Pedro de Osma, Bartolomé de Pareja, Alberto
de Rosa, &c.

It contains numerous examples of music, engraved on
wood.

x.

*Arte de Cāto llano 7 Cō | trapunto 7 Canto de
organo cō pro | porciones 7 modos breuemente
cō | puesta por Goçalo martinez de biz/cargui:
endreçada al muy magnifi/co 7 Reuerendo
señor dō fray Pas/qual obispo de Burgos mi
señor.*

At the end: ❡ " Esta presente arte de canto llano
nueuamente corrigida 7 añadida ciertas consonancias:
signos 7 mutāças por el mesmo Gonçalo martinez de
Bircargui. Fue empressa en la muy noble y leal cibdad
de Burgos por Fadrique aleman de Basilea, a iij dias de
abril. Año de ñro saluador Jesu xp̄o de mill y d-y-xj años."

4ᵗᵒ·. Black letter. 20 unnumbered leaves. Bibl. de
Toledo, 3ª, 2, 4.

A treatise of Theoretical Music. It contains a number
of wood engravings; among them the geometrical figure of
the division of the Diapason, also the explanation of the
intensity of the *Diatessaron*, and several others.

Don Fray Pascual de la Fuensanta, to whom this book
was dedicated, was Bishop of Burgos from 1497 to 1514.

XI.

Arte de Canto llano y Contrapunto y Canto de Organo con proporciones y modos breuemente compuesta: y nuevamente añadida, y glosada por Gonçalo martinez de Bircargui enderecada al Illustre y muy R. Señor don Juan Rodriguez de Fonseca Arçobispo de Rosano y obispo de Burgos mi señor.

8vo. Black letter. 84 leaves. At the end : " Intonaciones segun uso de los modernos que hoy cantan y intonan en la yglesia Romana. Corregidas y remiradas por Gonçalo Martinez Bircargui. Imprimidas en Caragoça, Año de 1549."

The music is printed on a red tetragram.

There is another edition, "Burgos, por Fadrique Aleman de Basilea, iij dias de Abril, 1511."

XII.

Tractado breue de prin | cipios de Canto llano. Nuevamente com | puesto por Joannes despinosa : racionero | en la sancta yglesia de Toledo. Dirigido al | muy reuerendo y magnifico señor el | señor don Martin de Mendoça Arcedia | no de Talauera y Guadalajara.

8vo. Black letter. 24 leaves. No year or place is given where this book was printed.

XIII.

Cursus quatuor Mathe | maticarum Artium Libera | - lium : quas collegit | atque correxit ma | gister Petrus | Ciruelus Daro | censis | Theologus simul et philosophus. 1526.

XIV.

*Arte de principios de Canto llano en Español
nuevamente emmendada e corregida por Gaspar
de Aguilar, con otras muchas reglas necesa-
rias para perfectamente cantar, dirigido al
muy ilustre señor Don Pedro Manrique, obispo
de Ciudad Rodrigo, y capellan mayor de la
capilla de los Reyes nuevos de la santa iglesia
de Toledo.*

8vo. Black letter. 16 leaves.

XV.

*Arte de Canto llano y contra | punto: e canto de
organo : con propor|ciones e modos : breuemente
compues|ta: por Gonçalo martinez de Bir-
cargui, enderecada al muy magnifico e reuerendo Señor don Fray Pascual: obispo de
Burgos mi Señor.*

Caragoça, 1527. 8vo. 24 pages. Music engraved on
wood.

XVI.

*Comiença el libro primero de la declaracion de
instrumentos, dirigido al clementissimo y muy
poderoso don Joan tercero deste nombre, Rey
de Portugal.*

Impresso en Ossuna, por Joan de Leon. 1549. 4to.
Black letter. 145 pp.

XVII.

*Commença el arte Tripharia, dirigida, a la yllustre
y muy reverenda señora D^{na} Isabel Pacheco,
abadessa en el monasterio de Sancta Clara
de Montilla, por el Rev^{do} padre Fray Joan
Bermudo.*

Impresso en Ossuna, por Juan de Leon.   1550.

XVIII.

*Manae Cantica, vulgo Magnificat dicta, Psalmata
octo tetraphona, per Christophorum Moralem,
aliosque Musicos. Adiecta tonorum octo
singulorum symphona isometra cantus per
quatuor voces Harmonia ad Psalmum quem
libet accomodabile.*

Impressum Lugduni per Jacobum Modernum.   Mil.
D. L. (*sic.*)
Folio.   Printed music on 33 leaves.   There are 5 motets
by Morales;   two motets by Jacquet;   one motet by
Richafort.

XIX.

*El Primo Libro de Diego Ortiz Tolletano, nel
qual si tratta delle glose sopra le cadenze
et altre sorte de punti, in la Musica del Vio-
lone nuovamente posta in luce.*

Roma, 1553.

XX.

Comiença el libro llamado declaracion de instru-
mentos musicales, compuesto por Juan Ber-
mudo de la orden de menores . . . examinada y
aprovada por los egregios musicos Bernardino
de Figueroa y Christoval de Morales. 1555.

Impressa en la villa de Osuna, por Juan de Leon. 1555.
Folio, 150 pp.

XXI.

Arte de Canto llano . . . puesta y reducida nueva-
mente en entera perfection, segun la practica
del Canto llano. Va en cada una de las reglas
un exemplo pintado con las intonaciones pun-
tadas. Ordenado por Juan Martinez.

First edition, Alcala de Henares. 1512. Another is
quoted, Seville, 1560.

XXII.

Francisci Sa/linae Burgensis | Abbatis Sancti
Pancratii de Rocca Scaligna in regno Na-
politano et in Academia Salmanticensi |
Musicae Professoris de Musica libri septem,
in quibus eius doctrinae | veritas tam quae ad
Harmoniam quam quae ad Rhythmum per-
tinet, juxta sensus et rationis judicium
ostenditur et demonstratur.

Salamanticae | Excudebat Mathias Gastius, 1578.
Folio, 445 pp.

XXIII.

Arte y somma de Canto llano compuesta y adornada de algunas curiosidades por Juan Francisco Cervera Valenciano. Dedicada a Dⁿ Philippe de Austria, tercero desto nombre, Principe de las Españas nuestro señor.

Valencia : en casa de Pablo Patricio. 1595.

XXIV.

Vergel de Musica espiritual, speculativa y activa, del qual muchas, diversas y suaves flores se pueden coger. Autor el Bachiller Tapia Numantino. Tratase lo primero con grande artificio y profundidad las alabanzas, las gracias, la dignidad, las virtudes y prerogativas de la musica, y despues las artes de Canto llano, Organo y Contrapunto en suma y en theorica.

Burgo de Osma. Diego Fernandez de Cordova. 4ᵗᵒ. (XVIth Century.)

PRINTED MISSALS, RITUALS, AND CEREMONIALS OF THE ROMAN CHURCH, CONTAINING MUSIC.

———•◦•———

I.

Incipit liber processionum secundum ordinē fratrū predicatorum.

At the end : "In alma Hispalensi urbe hispanie civitatum est impressum per Meynardum ungat Alamanum et Stanislaum Polonum socios. Anno a Christi natali MCCCXCIIII."

4to. Black letter, printed in black and red music on tetragram. 114 leaves.

II.

❡ *Missale secundum morem ecclesie Cesaraugustñ.*

At the end : ❡ " Finit missale : sĉđm morem ecclesie Cesaraugustañ : Regnāte Illustrissimo : ac Reuerēdissimo dño : Dño Alfonso de Aragone : eiusdeȝ Metropolis Antistite : accurate : diligēterq̃ emēdatū : ac impressum Cesaraugustñ : Iussu ꝉt impensis Pauli Hurus Constantiniensis : Germanici. Anno salutis : Millesimo quadrigētesimo nonagesimo octauo. Nono Kalendas Decembris."

4to. Black letter, 16 leaves with the title-page and preliminaries. CCX folios + CXXXV. Numerous engravings representing figures of saints.

Printed in black and red, the examples of music are placed in the tetragram.

Bibl. de Toledo. Sala reservada. E, 1, C, 4.

III.

Missale mixtum alme | ecclesie toletane.

Fol. At the end : " Finit missale mixtum alme ecclesie Toletane : magna cū dili/getia perfectū ꝉ emendatu : per diputatos a capitło eiusdeȝ / sancte ecclesie, in eadem regali ciuitate impressum Jussu / ac impensis nobilis Melchioris gorricij de Nonaria arte / ac industria magistri petri haghēbach alemani. Anno sa/lutis nostro, 1499."

It contains 320 leaves vellum.

IV.

Missale mixtum secundum regulam beati Isidori dictum Mozarabes.

Fol. Black letter. At the end : " Ad laudem omnipotentis dei. Expletum est missale mixtum . . maxima cum diligentia perfectum et emīdatū per . . doctorem dominum Alfonsum ortiz."

Impressum in regali ciuitate Toleti Jussu dñi d Francisci ximenes. Impensis nobilis Melchioris gorricij Nouariensis, Per magistrum Petrum hagembach, alemanum. Anno 1500.

It consists of 478 leaves.

V.

❡ *Breviarum secundum regulas beati hysidori.*

At the end : "Ad laudem omnipotentis dei necnō virginis marie matris eius : oīm sanctorū sanctarūq̃. Expletū est breuiariū secundū regulā beati ysidori dictū mozarabes : maxīa cū diligētia p̄fectū 't emendatū p reuerendū ī vtroq̃ iure doctore dñɜ alfonsum ortiz canonicū toletanū. Imp̄ssum ī regali ciuitate Toleti. Jussu reuerēdissimi ī xp̄o p̄r̃is dñi. D. frācisci ximenes : eiusdē ciuitatis Archiep̄i : Imp̄esis nobilis Melchioris goricii Nouariensis. Per magistrū Petrū hagembach Alemanū. Anno salutis nr̃e Millesimo quingētesimo secundo die v° vicessima quīta mēsis octobris."

Folio. Black letter. 8 unnumbered leaves + CCCCXXXII leaves, and two of index at the end. Printed on vellum in two columns. Black and red ink, 42 lines in each page.

Bibl. de Toledo, 3ª, 15, 2.

VI.

Manuale Chori.

At the end : "Fuit ante impressum hoc opusculum politissimum in nobilissima civitate Salmāticensiū in officina venerabilis viri Joānis de Porras, finituq̃ ī decima nona die novēbris anno a nativitate Christiana MD.vj. multa cura ac diligentia semel iterum atq̃ iterū revisum et castigatū p fr̃atres minores de obsvātia covētus eiusdē civitat qui ē in pvincia Sci iacobi."

8ᵛᵒ. Black letter. Printed in red and black. Music on a pentagram. 240 leaves.

VII.

Missale toletanum.

4to. At the end : "Impressum est hoc missale opus Burgis in officina Frederici ex basilea Germaī : ducta at auspicijs perq̃ Reuerēdi in christo patris ac nobilissimi domini Do Francisci Ximenes. S. R. E. H. Sancti Balbini Cardinalis hispani ac Toletani Archiepī et Arnaldus guillelmus brocarius faciendū curauit. Absolutū est pridie K$^{l.}$ maij Anno christiane salutis M. D. xij."

It consists of 341 leaves, black letter, printed red and black.

VIII.

Intonarium Toletanum.

At the end : "Explicit compendiū intonationū toti|us anni secundū consuetudinē scti ec|clesie Toletane studiosissime corre|ctum et emēdatum. Iussu reverē|dissimi ac illustrissimi dñi D. F. Frācisci Ximenes de Cisneros Cardinal Hispanie : atq̃ eius|dē ecclie Toletani archipre|sulis. Impressus atq̃ abso|lutum in preclarissima universitate cōplutē | si idustria atq̃ soler|tia Arnaldi guil|lelmi Brocarii |. Anno dñi M. |d. XV. die vero XVII. Martii."

Folio. Black letter, printed red and black. Music on pentagram. 120 leaves.

IX.

Passionarium Toletanum.

At the end : "Explicit Passionariū cum Lamentationibus jeremie atq̃ Benedictione cerei paschalis et Euāgeliis nativitatis ꝉ epiphanie dñi : scdm usum alme ecclesie

Toletane metropolis verissime correctum : jussu illustrissimi dñi D. F. Francisci Ximenes de Cisneros Cardinalis hispanie et ejusdem ecclesie archipresulis Hispaniarum primatis. Impressum atq̃ absolutū in egregia academia Complutensi in officina Arnaldi guillelmi Brocarii. Anno a nativitate christi millesimo q̃ngētesimo decimo sexto quinto nonas Julii."

Folio. Printed on vellum, black letter ; red and black. Music on pentagram. 72 leaves.

X.

Missale alme ecclesie Toletane cū multis addi-tionibus et quotationibus.

4to. At the end : " Explicit missale mixtum magna cū diligentia perfectū et castigatū ipresuꝫ iussu ac īpensis nobilis Melchioris Gorricij de Nouaria 1517."

It consists of 308 leaves. Black letter, two columns. red and black.

XI.

Guillelmus Croianus Cardinalis Archiepiscopus Toletanus Hispaniarum primat. Episcopus Camaracensis. Diurnum dnicale vel poti⁹ ordinarium secundum usum alme ecclesie Toletane. Absolutū in academia cōplutensi: & in officina Arnaldi Guillelmi Brocarii artis impressorie artificiossimi. Anno dni MD. xix. pridie kal. Julii.

Folio. Vellum, black letter, printed in black and red. 142 leaves.

XII.

Ordinariū de administratione Sacramentorū cum
pluribus additionibus adeo necessarias scdm
ritū alme sedis maioricensis.

At the end : " Ad cunctipotentis eiusq̃ matris et spōse
honorē ordinarium sive manuale ad ritū inclite maioricensis
sedis explicit Excussum Valentie ex officina Johãnis Ioffre.
Anno incarnationis salvatoris domini nostri Jesu Christi
MDXVI. die vero xiij mensis novembris."

4to.. Printed on vellum, black letter, black and red.
Music on tetragram, 8 leaves of preliminaries, 138 pages
of text.

XIII.

Missale mixtum secundum ordine Primatis eccle-
siae: eliminatus q. antea: ac iam nulla ex
parte confusum: cui accesit ordo celebrandi
Missam cum officio Diaconi et Subdiaconi: ac
de vsu et distinctione coloris ornamentorum
omnia per viros in rebus ac Ceremoniis eccle-
siasticas peritos composita.

Folio. " Finit Missale iussu Reuerendissimi Dñi D.
Alfonsi de Fōseca Impressu Cōpluti. In edib⁹ Michaelis
de Eguia. Anno salutis nr̃e 1530.

It consists of 278 leaves. Black letter, printed in red
and black.

XIV.

Manuale Sacramentorum secundum vsum alme
ecclesie Toletane Noviter īpressum cum qui-
busdā additionibus vtilissimis.

4to. At the end: " Explicit Manuale Impressum in
preclara Compluten. achademia. In aedibus Michaelis de
Eguia. Anno domini 1530 pridie kalendas Januarii."

It consists of 137 leaves, black letter, printed in red and black.

XV.

Missale Romanum.

At the end: " Cesar august. in officina Georgii Coci Anno Christiane salutis 1531, XV. idibus novembris."

4to. Black letter in red and black, printed in two columns. The music on the tetragram, with 14 pages of preliminaries and 260 leaves. There are several engravings in the text.

XVI.

Missale Romanum.

At the end : " Georgius Coci Teutonicus . . . . . Caesaraugustae, 1532 quinto kalendas Junii ad finem usq foelici sydere perduxit."

4to. Black letter, red and black, printed in two columns. The music on a tetragram. 9 pages of preliminaries, and 242 pages. Engravings in the text.

XVII.

Passionarium.

A volume in folio, black letter, printed in red and black. The music is on a tetragram of red lines. This volume consists of 68 pages. At the verso of the last page : " Accipe | devote lector | nunc denuo impressam veram passionis dñi nr̃i Jesu Christi historiã : suo cũ multũ cõpetenti cãtu ornata. . . . In insigni Cesaraugustana ciuitate | cura opaq̃ Georgij coci Teuthonici. Anno Christi 1538."

XVIII.

Missale mixtum secūdū ordinē alme Primatis ecclesie Toletane : elimin⁹ q. antea ac iam nulla ex parte confusum : cui accesit ordo celebrādi Missam cū officio Diaconi et Subdiaconi : ac de vsu et distintione coloris ornamentorum omnia per viros in rebus ac ceremonijs ecclesiasticis peritos composita.

4ᵗᵒ. At the end : "Finit missale Impressum cōpluti : In edibus Joannis Brocarij 1539." It consists of 350 leaves. Black letter, two columns, red and black.

XIX.

Missale secundum ordinē Primatis Ecclesie Toletane.

Fol. At the end : "Finit missale . . . iussu Illustrissimi ac Reuerendissimi dñi D. Joannis Martinij Silicci : Impressum Compluti. In edibus Joannis Brocarij Anno M.D.L quarto Calēdas Octobris." It consists of 384 leaves, printed on vellum, two columns.

XX.

Manuale Saramentorum secundum consuetudinē sancte Ecclesie Garnateñ. accuratissime emēdatū. Anno m.d.X.Lij.

At the end : "Apud inclytam garnatam Anno salutis nostri millesimo quingentesimo secūdo x die mensis novēbris."

4ᵗᵒ. Printed in black and red, the music on a pentagram, 132 leaves. Black letter, numerous engravings in the text.

XXI.

Missale Cesaraugustanum.

At the end: "Ad eius gloriam et honorem qui sibi sacrificium laudis jussit immolari : qui in sui memoriam fieri voluit quoties cūq veri, vivi ac immaculati illius agni fierit oblatio : absolutum est hoc libri Missalis opus quo veram sacrificii offerendi rationem presbyteri docetur passu it auctoritate illustrissimi ac reverendissimi domini d Ferdinandi ab Aragonia Cesaraugusti Archiepiscopi, ipsiusq̃ oculatissimi presulis cura et examine ad aliorū multorum collationem non paucis in locis castigatum Typis deniq Petri Bernuy chalcographi diligetissimi excusam Cesarauguste Idibus Augusti, Anno domini 1552."

4to. Black letter, the music on a tetragram, 242 leaves, and 22 of preliminaries.

XXII.

Manuale Sacramentorum secundum vsum alme ecclesie Toletane nouiter impressum, cum quibusdam additionibus vtilissimis.

4to. At the end : "Apud inclytam granatam, 1554." It consists of 151 pages.

XXIII.

Agenda Defunctorum.

On the verso of the title-page : " El Rey. Por quanto por parte de vos Juan Vazquez musico natural de la ciudad de Badajoz me ha sido hecha relacion que vos aveys hecho un libro de musica en que se contiene los maytines de difuntos y otras obras compuestas por punto de organo intitulado Agenda Defunctorum."

This volume contains all the Psalms used in the office

for the dead.   Folio, 62 leaves.   On the last page :
"Excudebat Hispali Martinus a Montedoca año [sic]
domini M.D.L. vj."

XXIV.

Enchiridion sive Manuale Chori quo brevitate ac
elegātia delucida, non solum divinum officium,
sanctae solenitatis, annuae Processiones, sta-
tutae gratulationes, funebris exequiae, piae sa-
creque ceremoniae, pro ut communiter Romana
praecipit Ecclesia, continentur ; sed omnia
prorsus quae ad ejusdem ritum pertinentia
non paucos latebant & diffusi vagabantur,
miro ordine studiosoq. labore congesta habentur.

Salamanticae apud Joannem a Canova.   MD.LVII.

XXV.

Processionarij Toletani prima pars.   Ad vsum
huius alme ecclesie cum processionibus et
officijs nempe dominicarum | festorūq. mo-
bilium : et aliorum.   Diligenter ordinata per
Joannem Rincon.

4to.   Toleti.   Exc. Joannes de Ayala 1562.   200 leaves,
black letter, black and red.

XXVI.

Manuale Chori secundum usum sanctae Romanae
ecclesiae.

Salamanticae. Apud Joannem a Canova M.D.LXIIII.
8vo.   Black letter, red and black.   Music on pentagram.
297 leaves, 7 of Index.

XXVII.

Liber processionarius regularis observantiae ordinis Cisterciensis in Hispaniarum regnis jussu capituli provincialis nuper correctus.

Salamanticae. Apud Johannem Baptistam a Terranova. Anno Domini 1569.

XXVIII.

Ordinarium Barcinonense Gulielmi Cassadori Episcopi iussu aeditum & in sex libros digestum, quibus ea continentur, quae potissimum ad parochi munus spectant Barcinone.

Apud Claudium Bornat.   Anno 1569.   4to.

XXIX.

Processionarium monasticum secundum consuetudinem congregationis Sancti Benedicti Vallisoletani.   Iam denuo auctum & emendatum.

Salmanticae.   Excussum cum licentia per Mathiam Gastium.   Anno 1571.

8vo.   Black letter, printed in red and black.   Music on a pentagram, 8 leaves of preliminaries, and 247 of text.

XXX.

Manvale ad Sacramenta Ecclesiae ministranda.

4to.   Salmanticae.   Ap. haered. Math Gastij.   1583.   It consists of 331 leaves, printed in red and black.

XXXI.

Passionarium cum officio maioris hebdomade juxta formam missalis et Breviarii Romanii ex decreto sacro Sancti concilii Tridentini restituti, cum canto Sancti Ecclesie Toletane: Joannes Roderici de Villamaior Portionarii Claustriq. in eadem ecclesie prefecti industria et labore recognitum.

Toleti. Excudebat Joannes a Plaça Typographus Sancte Ecclesie Toletane.   Anno incarnationis dñi MDLXXVI.
Folio. Black letter, printed in red and black. Music on a pentagram, 208 leaves.

XXXII.

Officium et coeremoniae ad dedicationem seu consecrationem Ecclesiae & ad consecrationem Altaris quae sit sine dedicatione Ecclesiae et ad reconciliationem Ecclesiae et Coementerii.

Omnia desumpta ex pontificiali Romano Matriti apud Thomam Juntam, 1595.
4to.   Printed in Roman letters in two tints, red and black, 210 leaves.   Music on pentagram.   Printed on purpose for the consecration of the Escorial.

PRINTED INSTRUMENTAL MUSIC.

——◦◦——

I.

*Libro de mu/sica practica. Compuesto por | Mos*ⁿ *francisco Touar: di/rigido al illustrissimo y | reverendissimo senyor | do Enrique de Cardoā| Obispo de Barcelona | y a su insigne | capitulo.*

La presente obra fue compuesta por mosen Francisco to|uar de la villa de Parcia. Imprimida en la insigne| cibdad de Barcelona por maestro Johan Rosen|bach aleman a V. de Janero anyo do mil y quinientos y diez.

II.

Libro de musica de vihuela de mano, intitulado el Maestro. El qual trahe el mesmo estilo y orden que un maestro traheria con un disci-pulo principiante: mostrandole ordinadamente desde los principios toda cosa que podria ignorar para entender la presente obra. Compuesto por Luys Millan. 1535.

Valencia por F. Diaz Romero.   Folio, black letter.

III.

Tractado de canto mensurable: y con/trapuncto: nueuamente compuesto por Matheo | de arāda maestro en musica.

Dirigido al mui / alto y illustrissimo sennor don Alonso

Cardinal / Infante de Portugal, Arcobispo de Lixboa /
Obisco Denora.

At the end: "Fue impressa la presente obra. En la
muy noble y semp. leal ciudad de Lisboa por German
Gailhard, Emprimedor. Acabose a los quatros dias del mes
de Setiembre. De mil y quientos : y treynta y cinco."

IV.

*Tractado d'cato llano nueuamente / compuesta por
Matheo de arāda maestro / en musica.*

Dirigido al muy alto y illustrissi/mo señor don Alonso
Cardinal Infante de / Portugal, Arcobispo de Lixboa,
Obispo / Denora comendatario de Alcobaça / com priuilegio
real.

At the end : "Fue impressa la presente obra en la muy
noble cibdad de Lixboa por German Gallarde : a veynte
y seys de Setiembre anno de mil y quinientos y treynta y
tres."

V.

*Los tres libros de musica de cifra para viguela.
Alfonso Mudarra.*

Sevilla.   1546.

VI.

*Libro de musica de vihuela intitulado Silva de
Sirenas.*

Valladodid.   Francisco Fernandez de Cordova.   1547.
Folio, 113 pp.

VII.

*Libro de musica de vihuela, agora nuevamente com-
puesto por Diego Pisador vecino de la ciudad
de Salamanca, dirigido al muy alto y poderoso
señor Dⁿ Philippe, principe de España.*

Folio.   Impresso en casa de Diego Pisador.   1552.

VIII.

*Libro de musica para vihuela, intitulado Orphe-
nica lyra. En el qual se contienen muchas y
diversas obras. Compuesto por Miguel de
Fuenllana. Di/rigido al muy alto y muy
poderoso señor Dⁿ Philippe, principe de
España, rey de Inglaterra, &c.*

Sevilla, por Martin de Montesdoca.   1554.   Folio.

IX.

*Libro de cifra nueva para tecla harpa y vihuela,
en el qual se enseña brevemente cantar canto
llano y algunos avisos para contrapunto.
Compuesto por Luis Venegas de Henestrosa.*

Alcala : en casa de Joan de Brocar.   1557.

X.

*Los seys libros del delfin de Musica para tañer
viguela.*

Por Luis Narvaez.   Valladolid.   1558.

XI.

Libro llamado Arte de tañer Fantasia, assi para Tecla como para vihuela y todo instrumento en que se pudiere tañer a tres y a quatro voces y a mas.

Compuesto por el muy reverendo Fr. Thomas de Santa Maria.

Valladolid, por Francisco Fernandez de Cordova. 1565. Folio, black letter.

XII.

Libro de musica en cifra para Vihuela intitulado el Parnasso, en el qual se hallara toda diversidad de Musica, assi Motetes, Sonetos, Villanescas en lengua castellana. Hechos por Estevan Daça vecino de Valladolid.

Por Diego Fernandez de Cordova. 1576.

XIII.

Magnificat | Moralis Ispani | cum quatuor vocibus.

Venetiis. Apud Angelum Gardanum. 1583.

4to. Printed music, containing 8 Magnificat and 8 Et Exultabit in each of the 8 volumes.

Cantus, Altus, Tenor, Bassus.

XIV.

Guitarra Española y vandola.

Por Carlos Amat. Barcelona. 1586.

XV.

Canciones y Villanescas Espirituales, de Francisco Guerrero, Maestro de Capilla y Racionero de la sancta yglesia de Sevilla a tres y a quatro y a cinco voces.

Venetia: en la emprenta de Iago Vincentio. 1589. 1 vol. in 4to, 41 pages with index of songs.

XVI.

Motecta Francisci Gverreri in hispalensi Ecclesia Musicorum praefecti. Qve partim quaternis, Partim Quinis, alia Senis, alia Octones Concinuntur vocibus. Liber secundus.

Venetiis. Apud Iacobum Vincentium. 1589. 4to, printed in black and red.

XVII.

Motectorum quinque vocum D. D. Sebastiani Raval nobilis hispani Ordinis Obedientiæ S. Joannis Baptistae hirosolymitani. Liber Primus.

Romae. Apud Franciscum Coattinem. 1 vol. 4to. At the verso of the title-page is the list of the 28 motets the volume contains, and the dedication to Cardinal Alejandro Peretti, dated 1593. Printed music for Altus, Quintus, Bassus.

H 2

XVIII.

Guerrero Francisco.

Motecta | Francisci Gverreri, in Hispalensi Ecclesia, musicorum Praefecti, Qvae partim qvaternis Partim Quinis, alia Senis, alia Octonis, & de Duo|denis concinuntur vocibus.

Venetiis. Apud Iacobum Vincentium, 1597.

5 volumes of music. Cantus, Altus, Tenor, Bassus, & Quintus. At the verso of the title-page there is a wood engraving representing the Crucifixion, and three figures. On the second page appears the

Index Motectorum.

QUATUOR VOCIBUS.

Per signum Crucis	1	Ave Regina coelorum	19
Sancta Maria	2	Salve Regina	20
Canite tuba in Sion	3	Erunt signa in Sole	21
Ibant Apostoli	4	Cum audisset Johannes	22
Iste Sanctus	5	Beatus Johannes	23
Istorum Est	6	Ego vox clamantis	24
Similabo Eum	7	Simile est regnum coelorum	25
Virgines prudentes	8	Cum turba plurima	26
Exaltaba est	9	In illo tempore	27
Petre ego pro te rogavi	10	Ecce nunc tempus	28
Dedisti Domine	11	Ductus est Jesus	29
Quasi stella matutina	12	Clamabat autem	30
Beatus est	13	In illo tempore	31
Gloriose confessor Domini	14	Accepit Jesus	32
Sancta et inmaculata	15	Docebat Jesus	33
Dum aurora finem daret	16	Regina coeli	34
Dulcissima Maria	17	O Domine Jesu Christe	35
Alma Redemptoris mater	18	Caro mea vere est cibus	36

QUINQUE VOCIBUS.

Hoc est praeceptum meum 37
Hic est discipulus 38
O crux splendidior............ 39
Ave Virgo Sanctissima 40
Ambulans Jesus............... 41
Trahe me post &c 42
Prudentes virgines............ 43
In conspectu Angelorum ... 44
Recordare Domini............ 45
Virgo divino nimium......... 46
Elizabeth Zachariae 47
Magne pater Agustini 48
Dum esset Rex 49

O virgo benedicta 50
Gaudent in coelis 51
Hic vir dispiciens mundum 52
Signasti Domine............... 53
Quomodo cantabimus 54
Gloria et honore 55
Quis vestrum habebit amicum 56
Ascendens Christus in altum 57
Dum complerentur 58
Et post dies sex............... 59
Cantate Domino 60
Post dies octo 61
Beatus es 62

SEX VOCIBUS.

Tota pulchra es Maria 63
Hei mihi Domine 64

Simile est regnum coelorum 65
O sacrum convivium......... 66

OCTO VOCIBUS.

Laudate Dominum de coelis 67

O Altitudo divitiarum 68

DUODECIM VOCIBUS.

Duo Seraphin 69

Missa, Seculorum, Amen, A, 470

HYMNA.

Te Deum laudamus 71
Ave maris stella............... 72
Veni Creator optime......... 73

Pange lingua 74
Magnificat Primi 75

Each of the books, *Altus, Cantus, Tenor,* and *Bassus,* contain 60 leaves.

Cath. Seville, Bibl. Columbina. Est. G, G, Fab. 175, Nos. 22, 23, 24, 25, and 26.

APPENDIX.

—•◦•—

I.

Specimens of Signatures written in Visigothic Cypher.

IT has already been stated in the Introduction that Visigothic writing consisted of different alphabets, which were used in MSS. They consisted of small letters without capitals, generally adapted in drawing up documents, letters, etc., and three distinct cyphers, one of which was used at the same time for music and signatures. It is possible this cypher existed previously to the Xth century ; but the specimens which have reached us appear in signatures attached to documents of the Xth, XIth, and XIIth centuries ; the signs which appear in Visigothic music of the time are exactly the same.

Facsimiles are given of these signatures taken from documents proceeding from the monasteries of *Sahagun* and *Eslonza*, Castilla la Vieja, existing in the Archivo Historico, Madrid (*see* p. 103). Many of the letters are different to the Visigothic writing. This has led students to suppose they proceed from the Roman alphabet. Facsimiles are here given of the specimens hitherto known. One of them is a note, written probably in the XIth century, to a document existing in the Cathedral of Leon, which contains a Miscellany of Spanish Councils, Treatises by Holy Fathers, Letters, etc. This memorandum states that the book belonged to the monastery of Sⁿ Cosme & San Damian, in the province of Leon, in the valley of *Abeliar*, near the river *Torio*. It is written with red ink, and in characters similar to those used in cypher, and in music. Some letters belonging to a known alphabet are to be found among them.

In order to understand these facsimiles, an alphabet of this cypher is given, copied from " Paleografia Visigoda," by Dⁿ Jesus Muñoz y Rivero. Madrid, 1881.

Fig. 38.

ALPHABET OF VISIGOTHIC CYPHER.

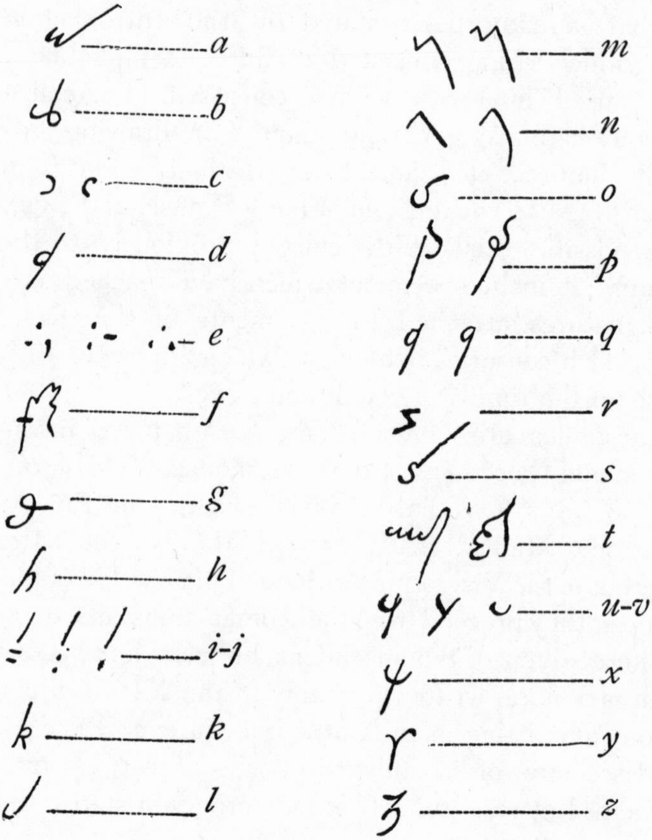

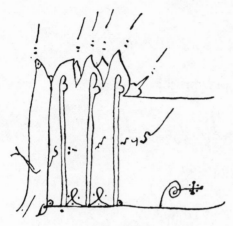

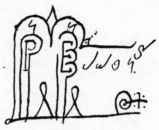

"PElagus."
(Bishop of Leon, A.D. 1081.)

"Petrus."
(Bishop of Astorga.)

"Petrus."
(In a document of A.D. 1081.)

"Pelagus."
(Bishop of Lugo, A.D. 995.)

gundisalbus notuit

adaulfus presuiter notuit

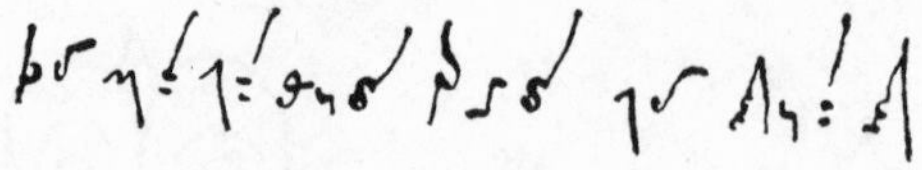

dominigus prs [presbiter |notuit

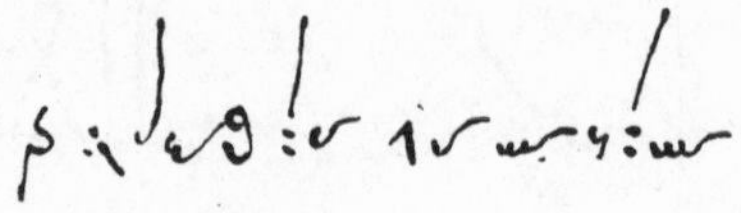

pelagio notuit

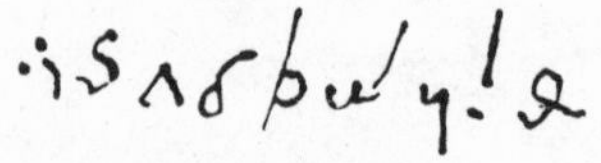

esnodavit [notavit]

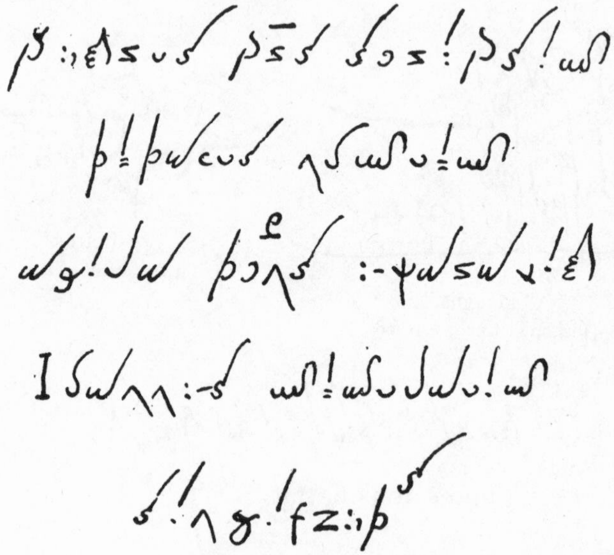

petrus pr̃s [presbiter] scripsit
didacus notuit
agila dc͡ns [diaconus] exarauit
Joannes titulauit
Singifred^{s} [singifredus]

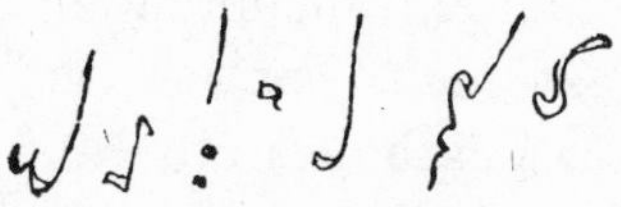

ariulfo

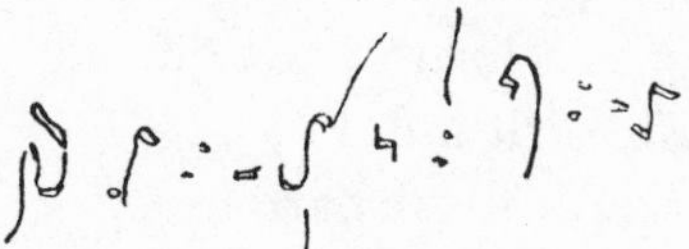

presuiter

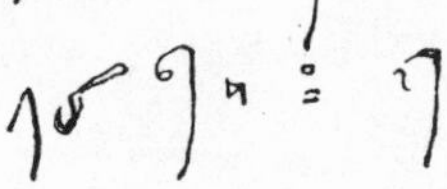

notuit

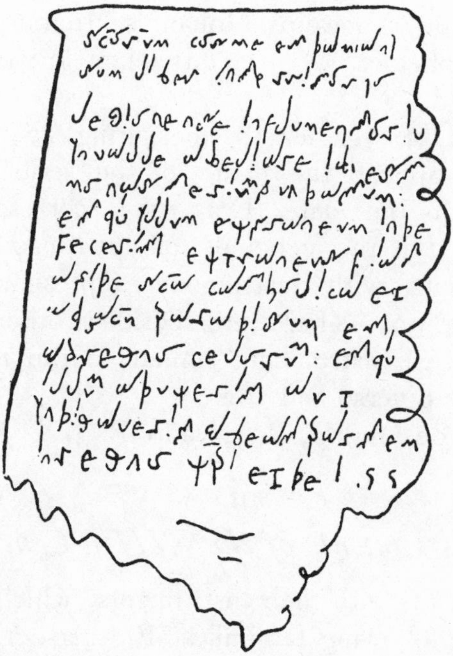

Scorum cosme et damiani
sum liber in territorio
legionense in flumen toriu
in valle abeliare . ibi est

monasteriuᵐ fundatum :
et qui illum extraneum inde
fecerit extraneus fiat
a fide sca . catholica et
ad sᵃcm. paradisum et
ad regno celoruᵐ. Et qui
illuᵐ aduxerit aut
indigaverit abeat partem
in regus xpi . et dei . s.s

II.

Musical Instruments of the XIth Century.

Tractatus de Apocalipsi Johannis. Item : Explanatio
Danielis Prophetae. Written on vellum in writing of the
XIth century.

It consists of 312 leaves, measuring 27½ᶜᵗˢ· by 19ᶜᵗˢ·
At the end appears the name of the scribe, *Facundus
scriptor*, with the date, Era 1085, corresponding to
A.D. 1047. On the verso of folio 272 may be seen the
seven musicians with instruments represented in the
facsimile, Fig. 39. There are, besides, other musicians
playing stringed instruments similar to the third in this
plate in folios 6 verso and 202.

Bibl. Nac. de Madrid, Reservado, B, 31.

III.

Musical Instruments of the XIIIth Century.

The musicians with their instruments, which are represented in the following facsimiles (Figs. 40–51), are taken
from the Codex of the *Cantigas de Santa Maria.* The
description will be found of this Codex among *Manuscripts
containing music.*

The plates are taken from Don F. Aznar's " Indumentaria Española," now coming out in Madrid. 1880.

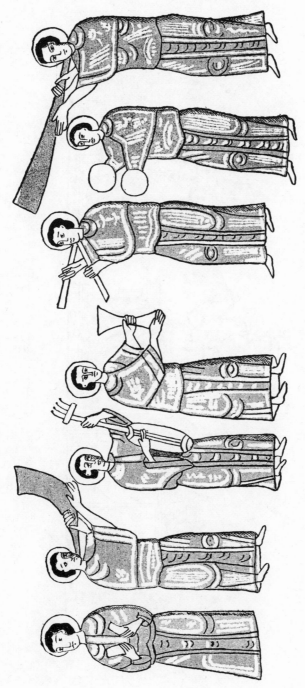

Fig. 39.—MUSICAL INSTRUMENTS OF THE ELEVENTH CENTURY.

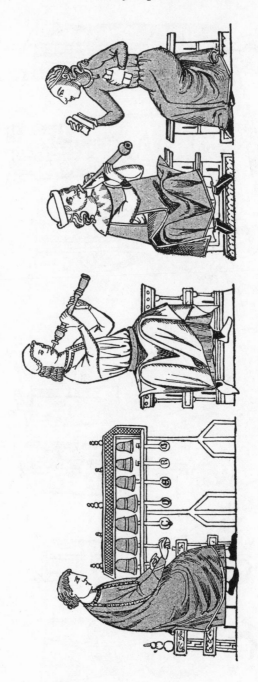

Fig. 40.—MUSICAL INSTRUMENTS OF THE THIRTEENTH CENTURY.

Fig. 41.—MUSICAL INSTRUMENTS OF THE THIRTEENTH CENTURY.

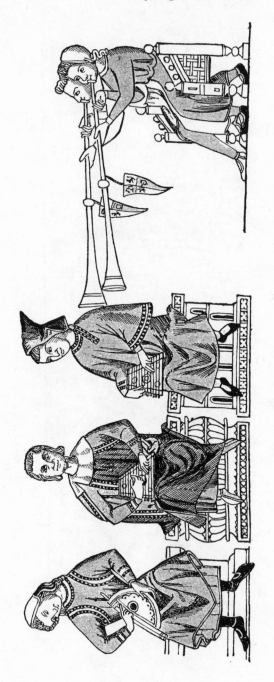

Fig. 42.—MUSICAL INSTRUMENTS OF THE THIRTEENTH CENTURY.

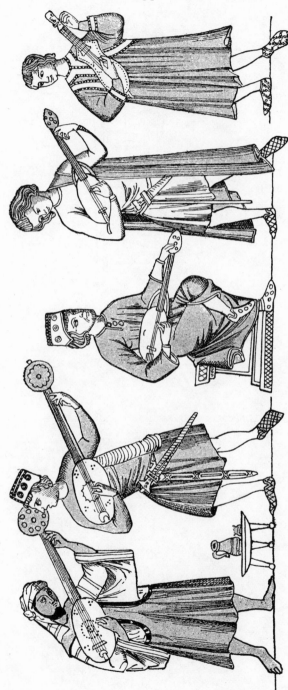

Fig. 43.—MUSICAL INSTRUMENTS OF THE THIRTEENTH CENTURY.

Fig. 44.—MUSICAL INSTRUMENTS OF THE THIRTEENTH CENTURY.

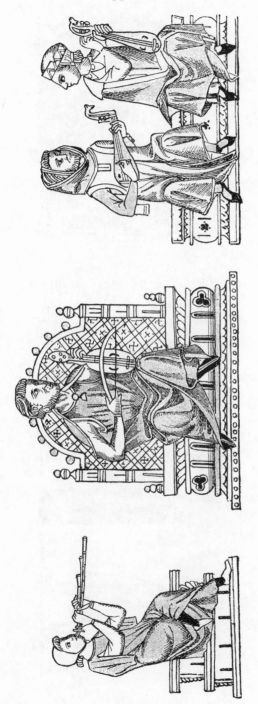

Fig. 45.—MUSICAL INSTRUMENTS OF THE THIRTEENTH CENTURY.

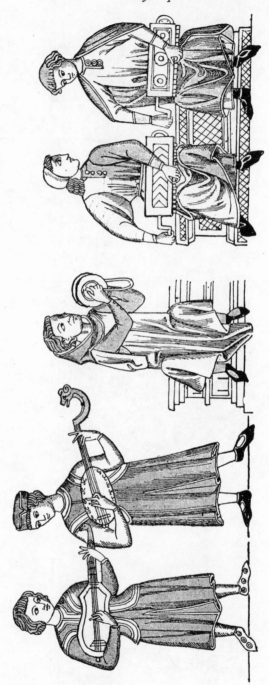

Fig. 46.—MUSICAL INSTRUMENTS OF THE THIRTEENTH CENTURY.

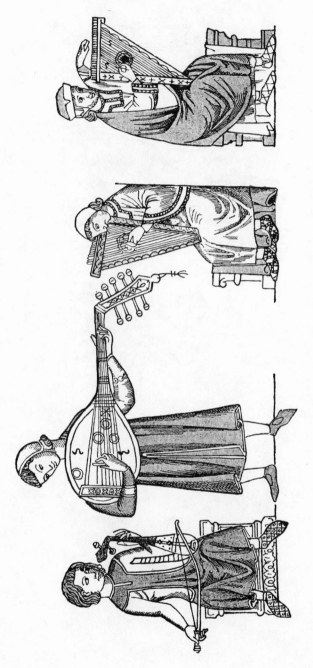

Fig. 47.—MUSICAL INSTRUMENTS OF THE THIRTEENTH CENTURY.

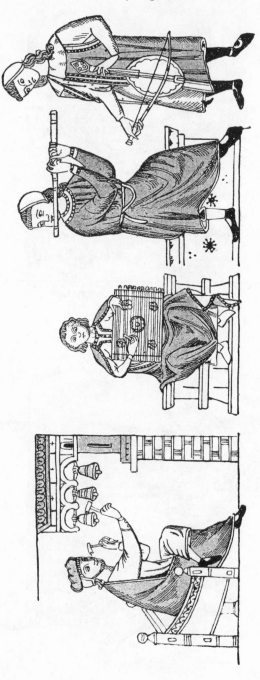

Fig. 48.—MUSICAL INSTRUMENTS OF THE THIRTEENTH CENTURY.

Fig. 49.—MUSICAL INSTRUMENTS OF THE THIRTEENTH CENTURY.

Fig. 50.—MUSICAL INSTRUMENTS OF THE THIRTEENTH CENTURY.

Fig. 51.—MUSICAL INSTRUMENTS OF THE THIRTEENTH CENTURY.

IV.

Libro de los juegos de agedrez, dados y tablas que mando escribir el rey Dⁿ Alonso el Sabio.

Written on vellum in characters of the 13th century, gr. folio. There is a contemporary memorandum at the end, stating that this MS. was written in Seville, by order of Dⁿ Alfonso, and was finished in 1283. It contains a number of miniatures representing the different games mentioned in the title; among them is a Moorish girl playing the harp. (*Vide* facsimile No. 52, Bibl. del Escorial, j, T, 6.)

Fig. 52.

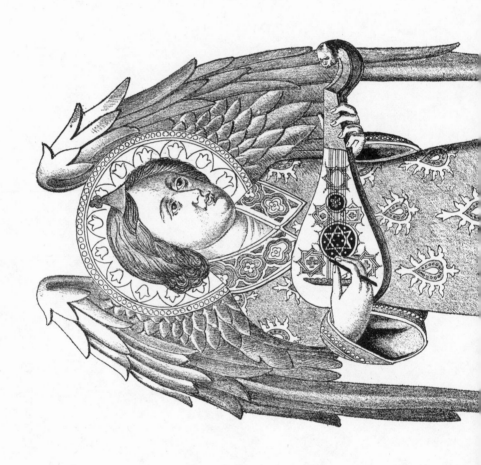

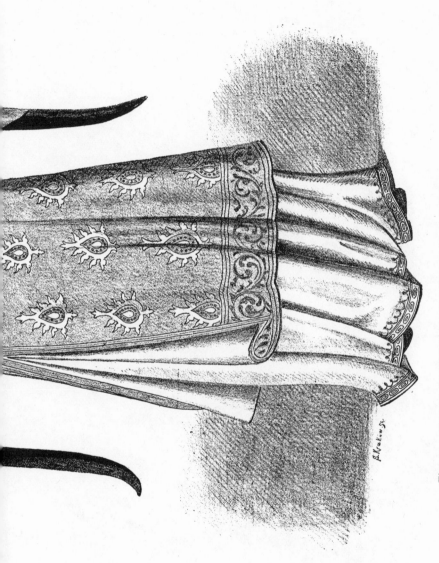

Fig. 53.—MUSICAL INSTRUMENT OF THE FOURTEENTH CENTURY.

v.

Musical Instruments of the XIVth Century.

At the Real Acad. de la Historia, Madrid, there is a very interesting altar-piece which was used to keep relics proceeding from the Cistercian monastery of Nuestra Sᵃ de Piedra, Aragon. It consists of a sort of cupboard with two doors, 2 mètres by 3 mètres, decorated with an ornamentation in relief, a mixture of Gothic and Arabic, and paintings in the Italian manner. Outside the doors are painted twelve subjects of the life of Jesus Christ and the Virgin; above, several sacred subjects, and coats of arms of Dⁿ Alonso II. of Aragon, and the Abad of the Monastery, Dⁿ Martin Ponce, who ordered this reliquary to be made. Inside the doors there are eight figures of angels standing and playing instruments. On two bands on the upper and lower parts of the doors there is an inscription in Latin, in Gothic letters, stating it was "depictum anno MCCCXC." (1390.)

The figures or facsimiles which are here given represent one of the angels (Fig. 53) painted on the doors, and six of the instruments held by the others (Figs. 54-59). These plates are published in "Indumentaria Española," by Dⁿ Francisco Aznar. Vol. I. Madrid. 1880.

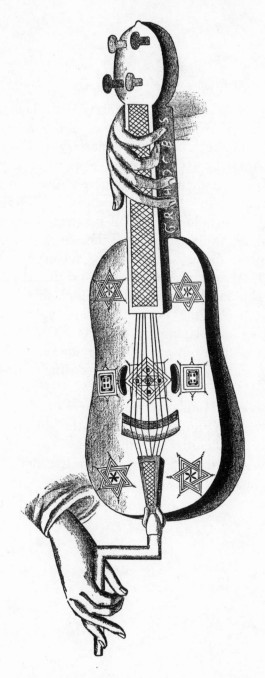

Fig. 54.—MUSICAL INSTRUMENT OF THE FOURTEENTH CENTURY

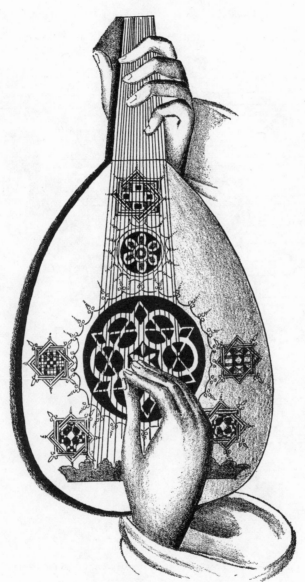

Fig. 55.—MUSICAL INSTRUMENT OF THE FOURTEENTH CENTURY.

Fig. 56.—MUSICAL INSTRUMENT OF THE FOURTEENTH CENTURY.

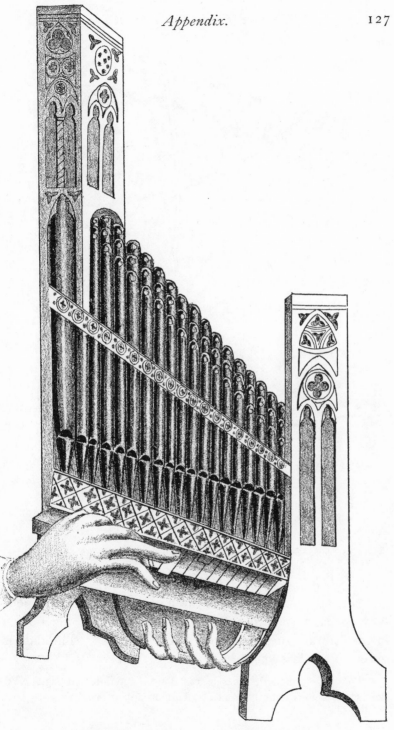

Fig. 57.—MUSICAL INSTRUMENT OF THE FOURTEENTH CENTURY.

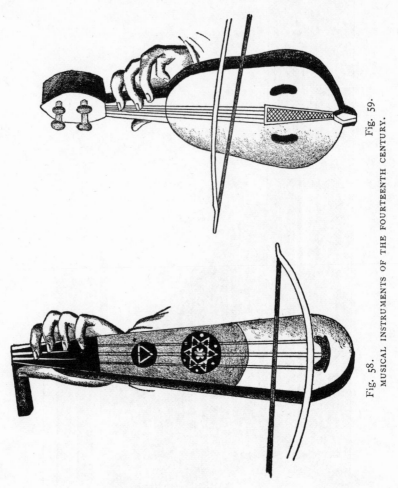

Fig. 59.

Fig. 58.   MUSICAL INSTRUMENTS OF THE FOURTEENTH CENTURY.

VI.

Names of the musical instruments which appear in a poem by Juan Ruiz, Arcipreste de Hita.

Juan Ruiz wrote towards the middle of the XIVth century, as we may gather from the MS. copy of his poems in the Library of the Cathedral of Toledo.*   The date is given in the last verse.

* *Vide* "Coleccion de poesias castellanas anteriores al siglo XV." Por Dⁿ Antonio Sanchez.   Madrid : Antonio de Sancha.   1790.

Era de mil é tres cientos é sesenta é ocho años fue aca-
bado este libro por muchos males é daños (1330).

These verses by Juan Ruiz are similar to a poem by
Guillaume de Marchant, "Prise d'Alexandrie," written also
in the XIVth century, in which a great number of musical
instruments are given.*

> Dia era muy santo de la pascua mayor,
> El Sol era salido muy claro é de noble color,
> Los omes, é las aves, et toda noble flor,
> Todas van rescebir cantando el Amor.
> Rescibenlo las aves, gayos, et ruyseñores,
> Calandrias, papagayos, maiores é menores
> Dan cantos plaçenteros, é de dulces sabores.
> Mas alegria facen los que son mas mejores.
> Rescibenlos los arbores con ramos et con flores
> De diversas maneras, de fermosas colores.
> Recibenlo los omes, et dueñas con amores,
> Con muchos instrumentos salen los *atambores.*
> Alli sal gritando la *guitarra morisca,*
> De las voces aguda é de los puntos arisca,
> El corpudo *laud* que tiene punto á la trisca,
> La *guitarra latina* con esos se aprisca.
> El *rabé* gritador con la su alta nota,
> Cabel el *garabi* tañendo la su rota.
> El *salterio* con ellos mas alto que la Mota.
> La *vihuela de pénola* con aquestos sota.
> *Medio caño* et arpa con el *rabé morisco,*
> Entre ellos alegranza el *galipe Francisco.*
> La *rota* dis con ellos mas alta que un risco,
> Con ella el *tamborete,* sin el no vale un prisco :
> La *vihuela de arco* fas dulces bayladas,
> Adormiendo á veces muy á las vegades.

* *Vide* the interesting pamphlet by Emile de Travers, "Les Instruments de Musique au XIV Siècle." Paris. 1882. 4to.

Voces dulces, sabrosas, claras, et tambien pintadas,
A las gentes alegra, todas las tiene pagadas.
Dulce *caño entero* sal con el *panderete*,
Con *sonajas de azofar* fasen dulce sonete,
Los *órganos* dizen *chansones* é *motete*.
La *citola albordada* entre ellos se entremete.
Gayta et *exabeba* et el finchado *albogon*
Cinfonia et *baldosa* en esta fiesta son.
El *francés odrecillo* con esto se compon,
La reciancha *bandurria* alli fase su son.
Trompas et *añafiles* salen con *atambales*,
Non fueron tiempo ha plasenterias tales,
Tan grandes alegrias, nin atan comunales,
De juglares van llenas cuestas é eriales.

(De como Clerigos é Legos é Flayres é Monjas é
Dueñas é Joglares salieron á recebir à Don Amor.)

VII.

Leges Palatinas.

King Dⁿ Jaime the third, of Aragon and Mallorca,
published in 1337 a collection of laws in order to organise
the members of his household. They are extremely interesting, for they give a good idea of the king's household,
from the highest to the lowest, the duties incumbent to
every one. From eighty to a hundred persons were
employed by him.

In the public library at Brussels there is a splendid
MS. of these *Leges Palatinas*, with miniatures which
represent eighty-seven members of the royal household,
each one with his different attributes. There are, besides,
many more illustrations, which are given at the heads of
the different chapters which divide the four parts of this
collection of laws. This MS. was published with com-

mentaries in the "Thesaurus Ecclesiasticae Antiquitatis,"
by the Jesuit Father Bollando, and exists in vol. i. page
421, of the work.

*Praefationes, tractatus, diatribae, etc. a Joanne Bollando
edita.* In folio. Venetiis. 1749. The facsimile given of
the king's musicians is taken from this edition.

In the last chapter (No. 28) of the first part of these
Laws, there are the following instructions to musicians.

DE MIMIS ET JOCULATORIBUS. R. XXVIII.

In domibus Principum, ut tradit antiquitas, mimi seu
joculatores licite possunt esse : nam illorum officium tribuit
lætitiam, quam Principes debent summe appetere, et cum
honestate servare, ut per eam tristitiam et iram adjiciant,
et omnibus se exhibeant gratiores.

Quapropter volumus et ordinamus, quod in nostra curia
mimi debeant esse quinque: quorum duo sint tubicinatores et tercius sit tabelerius ad quorum spectet officium,
quod semper Nobis, publice concedentibus, in principio
tubicinent; et tabelerius suum officium simul cum eis
exerceat, ac etiam idem faciant in fine comestione nostræ ;
nisi mimi extranei vel nostri qui tantum instrumenta sonant
in fine mensæ vellent Nobis volentibus instrumenta sua
sonare.

Ceterum nolumus quod in Quadragesima nec in diebus
veneris nisi festum magnum esset, dicti tubicinatores et
tabelerius suum officium faciant in principio mensæ nec in
fine. Alii vero duo mimi sint, qui sciant instrumenta
sonare ; et isti, tam diebus festivis quam aliis prout oppor-
tunum fuerit, instrumenta sua sonare debeant coram nobis :
Diebus tamen veneris Quadragesima, eo modo quo supra
dictum est, dumtaxat exceptis. Jubemus etiam quod
tempore guerræ, tam tubicinatores quam alii (nisi esset
mimus de tali instrumento quod tunc sonari non conveniret)
plus solito sint diligentes in officio, et ita nobis prope

existentes, quod cum opus erit promptos inveniamus ad suum officium peragendum Majores etiam domus sive Magistros hospitii ne vilipendant imo firmiter (eis) obediant.

Musici Regii

VIII.

MSS. with musical notes belonging to the monastery of Silos.

The ancient monastery of Santo Domingo, of Silos, in the province of Burgos, has been completely abandoned since the expulsion of the friars in 1835. A few years ago some French Dominican friars settled there, who have reorganised the archives and library. By verbal information given to me by one of the friars they possess the three following MSS.

Liber de virginitate Sanctae Marie et varia officia, written on vellum in the Era 1097, which corresponds with A.D. 1059. It contains music written with Visigothic signs.

Liber ordinum, written on vellum in the Era 1090, which corresponds with A.D. 1052. It contains music with Visigothic signs.

Ritus et Missae, written on vellum in the Era 1077, which corresponds with A.D. 1039. It contains music also with Visigothic signs.

The Bibl. Nationale de Paris possesses forty-two MSS. which were brought, in 1878, from the monastery of Silos. They have been minutely described by Leopold Delisle in " Mélanges de Paléographie et de Bibliographie." Paris. 1880.

Part of these MSS. belong to the XIth and XIIth centuries, and it is probable that the greater part have musical notes; but Mr. Delisle does not seem to have taken much notice of this, and to have principally studied their paleography. He only mentions " Leçons des Epîtres et des Evangiles des dimanches et des fêtes de l'année," p. 667, MS. on vellum, XIth century : " Antiennes, avec notation neumatique."

This MS. contains a memorandum written in 1067, stating it was given to the monastery of Silos. The donatario says he gives among others this *pneumato antifunario :* " Les Collations de Cassien," page 78, MS. on vellum, Xth to XIth century, " on a ajouté une prière a Saint Martial, *notée en neumes.*"

" Missal a l'usage de l'abbaye de Silos." MS. written on vellum at the beginning of the XIIIth century, page 113. " L'office de la messe pour le jour de la Conception est fort developpé et contient des parties *notées en neumes,* telles que le Kyrie avec farcissures."

IX.

Coleccion del Padre Buriel.

There is a series of 252 volumes in folio MSS. at the Biblioteca Nacional, Madrid, which was formed towards the middle of the XVIIIth century, by the learned Jesuit Padre Buriel. It contains copies of masses, breviaries, rituals, and a great number of ecclesiastical works taken from ancient MSS. of the Cathedral of Toledo, illustrated with commentaries and critical notes by Father Buriel, with the object of publishing an ecclesiastical library, which was never printed.   In order to give an idea of the writing of the original MSS., there are facsimiles by Palomares, a remarkable paleographer of the XVIIIth century.   Many of these reproductions have been copied from the originals without tracing.

In eight of these volumes there are facsimiles of music ; all the specimens given are of the Visigothic period, and belong to MSS. of the XIth and XIIth centuries.   As the originals exist in the Cathedral of Toledo, it is as well to know their titles and marks.

Officium totius quadragesimae.

Bibl. Nac. Madrid, Dd, 66, Cath. Toledo, 30, 8.

Officia et Missae de Tempore a Paschate usque ad adventum Domini.

Bibl. Nac. Madrid, Dd, 67, Cath. Toledo, 30, 3.

Psalterium integrum.

Bibl. Nac. Madrid, Dd, 69, Cath. Toledo, 30, 1.

Missale Muzarabe quadragesimale.

Bibl. Nac. Madrid, Dd, 71, Cath. Toledo, 30, 4.

Officia et Missae, XIth century.

Bibl. Nac. Madrid, Dd, 72, Cath. Toledo, 30, 5.

Breviarum cum Psalterium.   Item officium S. Leocadiae.

Bibl. Nac. Madrid, Dd, 73, Cath. Toledo, 30, 1.

Hymns for the whole year.

Bibl. Nac. Madrid, Dd, 75, Cath. Toledo, 30, 1.

Officia S. Martini et aliorum.

Bibl. Nac. Madrid, Dd, 79, Cath. Toledo, 29, 26.

X.

Memorias y disertaciones que podran servir al que escriba la historia de la Iglesia de Toledo desde el año 1085 en que la conquistó el Rey Don Alonso VI. de Castilla.

MS. in folio of 707 pp. The author was Don Felipe Fernandez Vallejo, canon of the Cathedral of Toledo, and afterwards Archbishop of Santiago. He wrote this MS. in 1785. It is divided in " Disertaciones." In the Vth and VIth he treats of the history of the music in the cathedral of Toledo. In the Vth chapter he says he has an objection to enter into the study of the ancient musical notes, but he gives interesting details on the manner of chanting *Canto llano*, the *Eugeniano* or *Gregoriano*, and the organs used from the XIth century until his time. The details that he has collected for the history of music are taken from the archives of the cathedral. In chapter VI. he writes : *Sobre las Representaciones poeticas en el Templo y Sybila de la noche de Navidad.* He copies an interesting poem translated from the Latin in Spanish verse of the end of the XIIIth century on the Sybil and Shepherds on Christmas eve, with its music. Several examples are also given of the music which served in the dramatic representations which were given in olden times in the Cathedral of Toledo. Although this MS. was written in the last century, the details it gives are so valuable that it has been included in this collection. Biblioteca del Marques de San Roman, Madrid.

XI.

Choir-books of the Cathedral of Seville.

They contain the music for the masses and feasts of the year, and form a most interesting collection, owing to the artistic beauty of the miniatures, borders, and fine capital letters. They are even more varied and beautiful than the collection of books at the Escorial. All of them are written on vellum.

There are upwards of 200 volumes, which may be divided into three groups :—1st. A collection of 107 volumes, which belong, by the character of their ornamentation, to the Gothic style used in Spain at the end of the XVth century : to the Renaissance of the XVIth century, and the decline of art in the XVIIth century. They measure 97$^{cts.}$ by 66$^{cts.}$. Those that belong to the Gothic style are the finest; they are 52 in number. 2nd. Another collection of 84. volumes, ornamented with fine Moorish designs combined with Gothic letters. They are 63$^{cts.}$ by 44$^{cts.}$. XVth century. 3rd. Several volumes which correspond to a later date, and less important.

All the music is written in black on pentagrams of red lines. The chapter ordered, in 1613, that a priest at Seville, Sebastian Vicente de Villegas, should correct the music in the manner of the Missal and Breviary reformed by Pope Clement VIII. He was two years doing it, and corrected 140 volumes of chants.

Some of the names of the artists who illuminated these volumes are known. They were Bernardo de Orta and his son Diego, Luis Sanchez, Andres Ramirez, and Padilla.

XII.

Choir-books belonging to the Monastery of San Lorenzo del Escorial.

They contain the music for the masses and feasts of the year. The collection is very important and numerous, and is splendidly ornamented. The music and liturgy is copied from the rituals of Toledo. King Philip II. ordered these books to be written in 1572, seventeen years were employed in writing and illuminating these volumes. They were finished in 1589.

They consist of 216 volumes on splendid vellum, measuring 1$^{m.}$ 15$^{cts.}$ by 84$^{cts.}$. They are bound in wood, covered with leather, and fine gilt brass ornaments; 5,500 pounds of bronze were used, and forty pounds of gold to gild these ornaments.

Each volume consists of seventy leaves, making a total of 15,000. The pages on which the music is written have only four lines, those without music ten lines. Every leaf is splendidly illuminated. At the beginning of some of the Introits and Antiphons there are fine illuminations which measure thirty and forty centimètres. The volumes are full of ornamented letters and borders.

The artists and scribes who wrote and illuminated these volumes were Cristobal Ramirez, Fray Andrés de Leon, Fray Julian de Fuente de el Saz, Ambrosio Salazar, Fray Martin de Palencia, Francisco Hernandez, Pedro Salavarte, and Pedro Gomez. The canon of the Cathedral of Toledo, Juan Rodriguez, undertook to correct the chants in 1581, and the red dots were added in the XVIIIth century by Fray Diego del Casar, master of singing in the Monastery.

Another corrector, Fray Ignacio Ramoneda, who lived also in the XVIIIth century, wrote an Index of these

Choir-books, in which numerous details are given of the cost of these volumes, bindings, cases to hold them, &c. This Index exists in the Library of the Monastery. H, iii, 26. One vol. 4to.

XIII.

Missa Gothica seu Mozarabica et officium itidem Gothicum diligenter ac dilucide explanata ad usum percelebris Mozarabum sacelli Toleti a Munificentissimo Cardinali Ximenio erecti et in obsequim Ill^{mi} perinde ac venerab. D. Decani et Capituli Sanctae Ecclesiae Toletanae Hispaniarum et Indiarum primatis.

1 vol. fol. Angelopoli, 1770 (Puebla de los Angeles), 198 pp.

Here follow the "Explanations ac Dilucidationes" of this volume by D^n Francisco Antonio Lorenzana, Archbishop of Mexico, and D^n Francisco Fabian y Tuero, Bishop Angelopolitanus ; both proceed from the Cathedral of Toledo. They were written during the stay of Cardinal Lorenzana at Toledo, who was anxious to imitate Cardinal Cisneros in giving importance to the Muzarabic ritual over the French or Roman one. This volume is extremely rare. Page 79 gives an explanation of the Muzarabic notes which are used in music. It cannot be affirmed that the opinions of the author are the exact and correct ones ; but this study, and one by D^{n}Jeronimo Romero, are the only two which have come to my knowledge, made in the XVIIth century, to interpret this music; they always must serve as a foundation for modern studies on this subject, for they are based on the traditions of the Cathedral of Toledo.

This explanation is headed by a rough engraving which is referred to in the text (*vide* facsimile, Fig. 60).

Fig. 60.

Verba hæc cum Notis Musicæ et Caracteribus Gothicis excerpta fideliter sicut ex Missali Muzarabum manuscripto, quod asservatur in Bibliotheca Toletana Scrinio 30, Num. 2, in Missa, quæ denominatur *Mediante die Festo* ad confractionem Panis.

Et ut figuræ Musicæ cognoscantur, simulque ad Notas nostri temporis eodem valore reducantur, advertendum prius est, sæculo nono (quod redolere videntur tam ipsi Caracteres, quam Notæ) Cantum Clave et tempore caruisse, et Cantores ad Vocis concentum dirigi a Systemate maximo certis signis, quibus dignoscebantur quando ascensus, vel descensus Vocis fieri deberet: Aliquando lineis rubri, et cærulei coloris utebantur, et aliquando absque lineis, jam per ipsam Notarum distantiam, jam per Magistri Vocem prius auditam dirigebantur: Ob hoc fatendum merito est, cantum illis temporibus non ad certas Regulas, Lineas et Claves ut hodie, fuisse adstrictum, imo rudem et informem dici posse quoad Notas, licet cantus revera melodicus et suavis esset.

His igitur prælibatis, clavis *Fēfaut* assignatur cantui Missæ *Mediante Festo* hac scilicet ratione, quia cantus ascendit ultra *La, Mi, Re.* Et ob hoc in tertia linea collocatur, ut detur locus absque augmento·ascensui de *Cc, Sol, Faut.*

Primum punctum hujuscemodi figuræ ❧ æquivalet *Fa* semibrevi, quia antiquitus ita figurabatur semibrevis solutus.

Secundum punctum hujuscemodi figuræ *∤* æquivalet *Mi* semibrevi soluto, ita etenim appingebatur.

Tertium et quartum sequentis figuræ ⟨⟩ æquivalent quinque punctis ligatis, ex iis primum et secundum sunt *Fêfaut, Gesolreut,* et *Fêfaut.* Quatuor priora minima sunt propter ligamen, quintum seu ultimum est semibreve propter descensum et syllabæ finem.

Quintum hujus figuræ ⌣ supponit tres seminimas, scilicet, *Elami, Fêfaut,* et *Elami.*

Sextum hujus figuræ ❙ est semibreve *Elami.*

Septimum hujus figuræ ➤ æquivalet tribus punctis ligatis, scilicet, semibrevi *Fêfaut,* et *Gesolreut,* et *Fêfaut* seminimis, ex eo quia statim sequuntur alia quatuor seminina.

Supra verbum *Festo* decem et septem puncta enumeramus in sequentibus figuris.

Primum est *Elami,* secundum *Fêfaut,* tertium *Gesolreut,* quartum *Elami,* omnia hæc semimina, quintum est cum nota semibrevis, et æquivalet tribus punctis, videlicet, *Fêfaut* semibrevi, et *Gesolreut,* et *Fêfaut* seminimis Sextum ➤ æquivalet alis tribus punctis ligatis, scilicet, *Gesolreut* seminimo, *Fêfaut* minimo, et *Gesolreut* seminimo. Septimum ⟨⟩ æquivalet quatuor punctis ligatis, scilicet, *Alamire, Gesolreut, Alamire,* et *Befabemi,* omnibus seminimis.

Octavum et ultimum hujus figuræ ⟨⟩ æquivalet tribus punctis ligatis, scilicet, *Cesolfaut, Befabemi* seminimo, et *Cesolfaut* semibrevi.

Nimis longum esset cæteras figuras explicare ; sat sit aliquas indicasse : Libenter recognoscimus nostram imbecillitatem ad Notas tam obscuras, et a nostro sæculo remotas declarandas : Nonulla etiam vitio et defectui scriptorum tribuenda sunt, et ignorantiæ nostræ parcendum.

XIV.

Breviarium gothicum secundum regulam Beatissimi Isidori, archiepiscopi Hispalensis, Jussu Cardinalis Francisci Ximenii de Cisneros prius editum ; nunc opera Exc^{mi} D. Francisci Antonii Lorenzana sanctæ Ecclesiæ Toletanæ Hispaniarum primatis Archiepiscopi recognitum. Ad usum Sacelli mozarabum.

Matriti, M.DCCLXXV, 1 vol., in folio.

The introduction, written by Lorenzana, follows the title. It is written with great learning, and gives most interesting details on ancient ecclesiastical rituals from the earliest times, pp. 1 to 25. The explanation given by D^n Jeronimo Romero of the Muzarabic chants will be found from p. 26 to 31. Fetis quotes this in his fourth volume of "Hist. de la Musique," p. 266. Romero discusses the theory of the Grecian tetrachord, and proves the necessity of using signs in every period, and the value of some of the Visigothic signs. He resolves the difficulties which might occur, and establishes the four rules here copied to understand the Muzarabic chants. His study is accompanied by the following facsimile :—

Fig. 61.

Cantus Eugeniani seu melodici explanatio. Facta a D. Hieronymo Romero, S. Ecclesiæ Toletanæ Hispaniarum primatis Portionario, et Cantus melodici Magistro.

REGULA Iᵃ.

Muzarabicus seu Gothicus cantus semper est mixtus, regiturque sub consideratione temporis, sive mensuræ binariæ, præter hymnos, qui sunt sub ternaria mensura : et ad pleniorem intelligentiam aspice signa textus superius assignati.

IIᵃ.

Omnes figuræ solutæ, licet diverso modo adpunctae, ut in num. 1 et 2, semibreves sunt, et uniuscujusque valor unum est tempus, seu mensura.

IIIᵃ.

Figuræ aliis duabus aut quatuor ligatæ, ejus valorem diminuunt, et dimidiant; ita ut duæ ligatæ unam semibrevem componant : hoc patet in nostro textu, ubi num. 3, 4, 6, et 7, et in letteris M et Q, ea tantummodo differentia, quæ cernitur in num. 4, ubi ligat quatuor æquales figuras, quocumque modo sit locata ; et licet figuræ litterarum M et Q alias quatuor figuras singulæ ligent ; intelligendum est duas priores minimas, et alias duas semibreves esse : hoc apertius intelligitur sequenti exemplo. Quando nos hodie in tempore minori figuras duabas semibrevibus æqualiter ligatas videvimus, valorem duplicatum eis damus.

IVᵃ.

Figura quæ est sub num. 12 brevis est : primo quia ibi mediat versus : secundo, ut ibi requies aliquantulo fiat ad prosequendum cantum. Vltima figura, quæ est sub littera Q, etiam brevis est ; quia in ea finitur opus.

His accedit, me a puerulo instructus fuisse regulis cantus non solum plani, et figurati, sed etiam Eugeniani, seu melodici, ut vocant, qui usque ad nostram ætatem in hac Alma Toletana Ecclesia, Hispaniarum primate perdurat ita ut alternatim cum cantu Gregoriano mirabili consonantia permiscatur.

Romero is of opinion that the author of this mode of chant was Eugenio III., Archbishop of Toledo in the VIIth century, in *arte Musica peritissimus,* and ends by saying that whoever doubts his explanations ought to go to the Cathedral of Toledo, and will judge for himself how the system of chanting has been preserved from the earliest times.

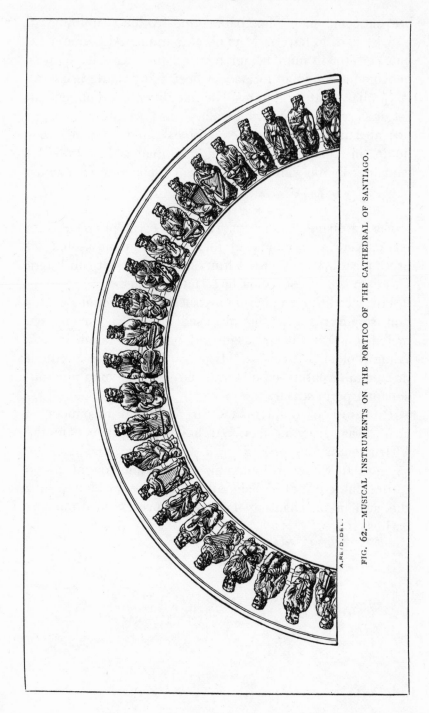

A. REID. DEL.

FIG. 62.—MUSICAL INSTRUMENTS ON THE PORTICO OF THE CATHEDRAL OF SANTIAGO.

XV.

Musical Instruments on Spanish Porticos.

Numerous examples exist in Spain of porticos of romanesque churches of the eleventh and twelfth centuries, on which may be seen the twenty-four elders holding musical instruments. One of the finest examples is at Santiago, *vide* Fig. 62. A reproduction of this portico, built by Maestro Mateo, may be seen at the South Kensington Museum. Worthy of special mention are the porticos of Ripoll and Toro.

The portico of the church of Ripoll (Cataluña) is one of the most splendid specimens of sculpture in Spain. The twenty-four elders hold lyres in one hand and chalices in the other. To the right of the portico there are five large statues of musicians, four of which are playing the flute, the horn, cymbals, and the violin. The fifth central figure appears to direct the others, and the whole composition represents the text of the 150th Psalm.

The northern doorway of the collegiate church of Toro (Castille) is also built in the romanesque style, twelfth century. The arch of this doorway is built in the wall, and contains four zones of ornamentation and figures which decorate the archivolts. The last zone, which is also the largest, is decorated with a series of figures which are placed on each side of the representation of our Lord, which is in the centre on the keystone. These twenty-six figures are arranged, thirteen on each side of our Lord. Two figures which are on the right and left are apparently local saints. The remaining twenty-four figures wear crowns, and hold musical instruments, and represent the elders of the Apocalypse.

GENERAL INDEX.

Ramirez, Christobal, illuminates the choir-books of the monastery of the Escorial, 137

Ramoneda, Ignacio, corrects the chaunts in 1581 at the monastery of the Escorial, 137

Ramos de Pareja, Bartholomé "De Musica Practica" by, 70

Raval, Sebastiani, composes a motet for five voices, 99

Raymundus de, Silva, Fr., "De doctrina finali fragmentum" by, 67

Reginon, a writer on musical annotations, 18

Ribera, Antonio, Spanish musician of the 16th century, 3

Ribera, Pedro de, Bishop of Lugo, to whom Molina dedicates his book "Lux videntis," 76

Riemann, Hugo, author of "Studien zur Geschichte der Notenschrift," 16

Rincon, Joannem, edits a volume on the ceremonies used in processions, 92

Ripoll, Cataluña, Monastery of, where a Latin poem on music existed in the 11th century, 7, 145

Ripoll, Cataluna, musical instruments on the Portico of Santa Maria de, 145

Ritual of the congregation of Perugia, 14th century, 53

Ritual, the Visigothic or Eugeniano, 6

Romero, Diaz F., printer at Valencia in 1535, 95

Romero, Jeronimo, an interpreter of Visigothic musical neums, 19, 138, 141, 143

Rosa, Alberto de, a musical composer mentioned in Marcos Duran's commentary on "Lux Bella," 77

Rossi, "Diz. Historico," commentator of Alfarabi, 42

Rota, musical instrument used in Spain in the 14th century, 129

Royal Library, Berlin, a MS. copy of Ramos de Pareja written in the 15th century, 72

Royal Library at Munich, MS. with neums in the, 18

Ruiz Juan, Arcipreste de Hita, writes a poem in the 14th century in which the names of musical instuments are given, 123, 129

Sacraments, instructions for the administration of, 16th century, 68

Sahagun, monastery of, from whence a number of documents with Visigothic signatures proceed, 103

Saint Gall, Antiphonaire, 17

Salavarte, Pedro, illuminates in the choir-books of the monastery of the Escorial, 137

Salazar, Ambrosio de, one of the scribes of the choir-books of the monastery of the Escorial, 137

Salazar, Manuel de, writes in 1775, an Index by order of Cardinal Lorenzana and the choir-books at Toledo, 24, 29

Salicus, 16

Salinae Burgensis, Francisci, author of a work on music, 81

Salinas, Bernardo, Spanish musician of the 16th century, 3

Salterio, musical instrument mentioned in a poem of the 14th century, 129

Salva, Jacobo, Fratre, "De pulsatione Lambuti," 10

Salvus, Abbot of Albelda, a musical composer, 7

Sambuca, 5

Sanchez de Tineo, Juan, a Spanish musician of the 16th century, 4

Sanchez, Luis, an illuminator of the choir-books of the Cathedral of Seville, 137

Sancho, Don, 9

Santa Maria, Fr. Thomas de, author of "Arte de tañer Fantasia," 1565, 98

Santiago, Cathedral of, musical instruments on the Portico of the, 144

San Lorenzo del Escorial monastery, choir-books belonging to the, 137

San Roman, Marquis of, owns a fine library at Madrid, 135

Santos, Juan, a native of Toledo and musician of the 16th century, 4

Scandicus, 16

Schelle, German critic on music, 3

Senis, Fr. Nicolaum de, musical works, 67

Silva, Fr. Raymundus de, musical works, 67

Singifred, Singifredus Joannes, in a document in Visigothic cypher, 106

Sistrum, 5

Sonajas de Azofar, musical instrument used in the 14th century in Spain, 130

Soriano Fuertes, Mariano, author of "Historia de la Musica Española des de la Venida de los Fenicios hasta el año de 1850, Madrid, 1885, 11

Soto de Langa, Francisco, a Spanish musician of the 16th century, 4

Spanish Royal Academy, is preparing an edition of the "Cantigas," 48

Spañon, Alonso, author of a work on Canto llano. 75

Stanislaus Polonus, printer in Seville in 1494, 83

"Studien zur Geschichte der Notenschrift," *vide* Riemann, 16

Sulpicius, Severus, 35

Symphoniam, 5

Talavera, Francisco, a Spanish musician of the 16th century, 4